Why Me, Lord?

*Biblical and Practical Answers
For Suffering in Our Lives*

WALLY LONG

WESTBOW
PRESS®
A DIVISION OF THOMAS NELSON
& ZONDERVAN

WestBow Press books may be ordered through booksellers or by contacting:

WestBow Press
A Division of Thomas Nelson & Zondervan
1663 Liberty Drive
Bloomington, IN 47403
www.westbowpress.com
844-714-3454

All Scripture quotations are taken from the ESV® Bible (The Holy Bible,
English Standard Version®), copyright © 2001 by Crossway, a publishing
ministry of Good News Publishers. Used by permission. All rights reserved.

ISBN: 979-8-3850-1488-0 (sc)
ISBN: 979-8-3850-1489-7 (hc)
ISBN: 979-8-3850-1490-3 (e)

Library of Congress Control Number: 2023923852

Print information available on the last page.

WestBow Press rev. date: 03/18/2024

Contents

Part 2. What Causes Our Suffering?

Part 3. The Purposes of Our Suffering

Foreword

A conversation on trials and sufferings does not usually elicit feelings of being welcomed, but that is exactly how this book felt. It felt like a hospitable, gentle invitation to sit with Wally Long and hear the deep groanings of his story's suffering and the depth of comfort that a rooted biblical perspective has given him. In a world where suffering is inevitable and some seem to experience it more than others, he does not approach this as someone who has all the answers and wants to preach at you. Instead, he invites you to join him as he wrestles with the question, "Why me, Lord?"

Chesed Anne Dent
Director of Global Studies Internships and Adjunct Faculty
Global Studies, Liberty University

Preface

Why Me, Lord?

On October 26, 2006, I received a phone call from my brother Cal. He told me that our youngest sister Tessie had shot herself and was dead. What? I could hardly believe my ears! We rushed to Nebraska to be with her husband and young daughter. The entire family was there. It was a very emotional time for all of us. Because of her self-inflicted wounds, her body had to be cremated, and we had a memorial service. Her husband asked me to preach the service. It was one of the hardest things I had done at that point in my life.

In the months following, I felt at fault. Tessie and I spoke on the phone just a few days prior to her suicide. As a trained professional, I had suicide awareness training. I should have picked up on clues during our phone call. I could have intervened and saved her life. Mom also felt responsible. She had attempted suicide by gun in 1972. She believed her example led Tessie to do what she did. The fact is, there was nothing anyone could have done. She found herself in some legal trouble over some things she had done in her past. Instead of telling us, she chose to go out on her own terms, and she did.

While we were still grieving my sister's death in July 2007, I received a phone call at about 12:30 p.m. from a worker in the ER at one of the local hospitals. One of my sons, who was then eighteen years old, had been in an accident on his motorcycle on the way to our house. She told us we needed to get to the hospital right away.

We arrived at the hospital to find our dear son in the ER screaming in pain. He had lost his right leg in the accident, lost a lot of blood, and nearly died. He spent two weeks in the hospital and had many surgeries. On the day we were taking him home, I received yet another phone call. This one was from my other sister in Colorado. Mom had been taken to the hospital and was dying. Mom's health had not been good for many years because of injuries she sustained in a suicide attempt when I was only twelve years old. Her injuries had finally gotten the best of her, and her body simply stopped functioning. She died a few weeks later on September 5, 2007. I never had the chance to say goodbye.

Our family was in a state of emotional, physical, and spiritual turmoil. I lost a sister, almost lost my son, and lost my mother in less than eleven months. I had been preaching as a layperson at a church we had helped to start, but I had nothing left to give, emotionally or spiritually. We left that church and started attending one closer to home so we could just rebuild and recuperate after months of intense trauma.

It took us a long while, but eventually, our life took on a sense of normalcy. Then on March 1, 2011, our world completely turned upside down. I was nearing the end of my shift at the federal prison in Springfield, Missouri, where I worked. At about 9:20 p.m., I received a phone call from my brother's oldest son. He was sobbing uncontrollably. Through his sobbing, he told me that someone had broken into his parent's house and killed them both. The attack injured their two youngest children, a five-year-old girl and a nine-year-old boy, and they were being life-flighted to the Children's Hospital in Denver.

I rushed to the airport and took a plane to Colorado, arriving early the next morning. The rest of my family followed by car arriving late the next evening. The next few days were a whirlwind of emotion and grief. For a while, it was touch and go for the boy. His injuries were severe. He had been shot twice and stabbed six times. The bottom completely fell out of our upside-down world two days later when the investigator told us they had arrested my brother's own twelve-year-old son for the terrible deed. No way! How could this be? But the case was rock solid. He had killed his own parents and almost killed his little brother and sister.

We spent almost six weeks in Denver while the two young children recovered sufficiently to be taken back to our home in Missouri. By necessity, I retired from my prison career at the end of April 2011. Over the course of the next several months, I made many trips back and forth to Colorado for both the adoption hearings (the state of Colorado was facilitating the adoption of the two children into our family) and the court hearings for the murder case.

The attorneys in the case ended up agreeing to a plea deal whereby the now thirteen-year-old boy would plead guilty to first-degree murder in juvenile court. In September 2011, they sentenced him to the maximum of seven years in prison. Two months later, in November 2011, the adoption was finalized, and my brother's two youngest children were now our seventh and eighth children.

In the years following, there was much counseling for both the two children and our youngest natural son, who was the same age as the nephew who killed his parents. My wife and I had been holding the family together and finally went into counseling to help us deal with the trauma and the changes forced upon us.

I found myself repeatedly asking, "Why me, Lord? Why have you allowed all of this tragedy to take place in my family?" I began to search the scriptures for answers, and God gave me a sermon. It was a sermon that I needed. It was a sermon born of deep grief and suffering. I have shared this sermon with many audiences in churches and other Christian events. That sermon became the idea for this book. I pray that the lessons I learned through our tragedies and my study of the Bible will be a blessing to you as you read this book.

Throughout this book, I will use various words to describe the tragedies we face in our lives—trials, tribulations, troubles, hardships, hard times, afflictions, storms, and sufferings. I will use these terms somewhat interchangeably to describe the difficulties we all face.

This book is not a Bible study although I will, throughout the book, define some biblical words in more detail to better explain how the word and the related passage help us answer the question, Why me, Lord? It is not a book of theology although my theological bent will be seen throughout the book. Please do not let differences in theology and doctrine prevent you from reading this book for the answers you need.

This book is also not a how-to book. I am not trying to give you a step-by-step plan for enduring or overcoming your trials and tribulations. There is no such plan. However, as I share with you the various aspects of *why me*, I will endeavor to give you biblical principles to help you through your dark time.

This book is a book of encouragement. I pray that the answers and biblical principles found in this book will encourage you while you are going through difficult times in your life. As I have found answers, I have written to help you find answers. I believe the answers found in the Bible and detailed in this book will help you get through the trials in your life.

I also pray it will help those walking alongside friends and family who are going through hard times. As we all know, it is hard to find the right words to say to someone who is suffering. Trite but true phrases such as *the Lord is walking with you, all things work together for good*, and other such phrases are usually not comforting in the middle of tragic circumstances. So what do you say? Just be with them. Hand them this book and encourage them to read it when they are able. Pray with them. Walk with them as they seek answers during their times of great hardship.

Acknowledgments

I hesitate to write my thanks to all those who have been a part of my life and helped me make this work a reality for I do not want to miss anyone. But I will do my best.

I want to thank my sweet wife Sylvia for walking through all the tragedies and trials we have faced in our life together. She has been a consistent source of love and encouragement. We have faced our storms together, drawing strength for each other in the love God has given us. Without her, I would not likely have found the courage to write this book.

I want to thank each of my wonderful children: Ashley, Austin, Aric, Alyssa, Alexander, Aaron, Ethan, and Sarah. In various ways, they have all taught me how to be a father. I know I have failed terribly many times, but their love for me has remained constant. I am the man I am today because of the influence of each of my children in my life.

I want to thank each of my dear friends who shared with me their stories of tragedy and suffering, allowing me to use their stories. I know it was difficult for them, but I pray their stories will help many others. To Lucinda, Glennis, Bethany and Gabe, Ben and Christina, and Rod, may God bless you all for sharing your stories with those who read this book.

I want to thank Bev and Dave for allowing me to use the lasagna story. Bev, I know it still embarrasses you, but know that God has used this story to encourage and bless many people throughout the years.

I want to thank Anastasiya Bolton for allowing me to use the story of our interaction in the aftermath of our tragedy. She has been a faithful friend.

I want to thank Chesed Anne Dent, my favorite professor in my recent journey of completing a degree I started in 1978. Her kind words of encouragement found in the foreword of this book meant a lot to me coming from someone I admire and respect.

Finally, and most importantly, I need to express my gratitude to God Almighty. I searched for answers to the questions of my heart, and He gave them to me. He helped me understand *why me* and I pray that the answers He gave me will bless all those who read this book.

Part 1

General Thoughts about Trials, Afflictions, and Sufferings

Introduction to Part 1

Before we can adequately attempt to answer the question of *why me*, we must first look at some basics concerning trials, tribulations, hardships, and sufferings. These basic concepts will help us frame a place in our hearts and minds for the answers we seek.

Nothing in this first chapter will be mind-blowing. It is likely you are already aware of each of these basic concepts. You may know them intuitively. You may have heard them in a sermon or read them in a book.

Take your time reading this first chapter. Pray that God will prepare your heart and mind for the answers He has for you from His Word.

Chapter 1

What Does the Bible Say about Trials and Sufferings?

Suffering Is Not God's Original Plan for Humanity

In Genesis 1 and 2, God created a perfect world. I believe He did it in six literal days. God saw that "it was very good" (Genesis 1:31). How long it remained in that perfect state, we do not know. But we know that Lucifer, God's most beautiful and powerful angel, rebelled against God's authority. He then began a campaign of terror and destruction in God's perfect world.

He tempted Adam and Eve to disobey God's commandments. They did and sin entered the world. God told Adam in Genesis 3:17–19, "Because you have listened to the voice of your wife and have eaten of the tree of which I commanded you, 'You shall not eat of it,' cursed is the ground because of you; in pain you shall eat of it all the days of your life; thorns and thistles it shall bring forth for you; and you shall eat the plants of the field. By the sweat of your face you shall eat bread, till you return to the ground, for out of it you were taken; for you are dust, and to dust you shall return." Adam would know suffering, and he knew it because of the evil actions of God's enemy, Lucifer, now Satan.

When sin entered the world through Adam, pain and suffering came right along with it. When sin entered the world through Adam, death accompanied it. Paul wrote in Romans 5:12, "Therefore, just as sin came into the world through one man, and death through sin, and so death spread to all men because all sinned." Pain, suffering, and death are the natural consequences of sin.

God created a perfect, sin-free world. It was a world absent of pain, suffering, conflict, tribulation, and hardship. It was a world of glory, peace, and wonder. This was the world God wanted for His people. But when Adam and Eve disobeyed God, the world began a headlong slide into chaos and self-destruction. Suffering followed closely behind. The suffering we all now experience was not God's plan for us. Death was not part of God's plan.

There will be more about this in later chapters. For now, just understand that we suffer because of the sin that entered the world through Adam's disobedience.

God Is Working His Plan to Eliminate Suffering

Theologians and philosophers could argue and debate much about the origin of sin and the effects of sin on God's creation. In fact, they have. But that is not something I wish to rehash in this short book. Just know this, all the pain, suffering, and death we experience in this life are a result of sin. God created Adam and Eve in a perfectly created world, yet they sinned. Death and chaos followed. But that does not mean God was caught off guard. When Adam and Eve sinned, God did not say in surprise, "Oh my! Adam blew it big-time! What am I going to do now?"

God gave Adam and Eve the free will to choose whether to obey God or disobey. They chose poorly, but God is a merciful and loving God. He did not utterly destroy them and start over. Instead, He set in motion a plan to redeem humankind and all of His creation. God did not abandon humankind to fend for themselves. Instead, He came down to earth to enter our suffering, pain, and chaos.

Jesus left the glory of heaven and the eternal communion He had with the Father and the Holy Spirit to be born of a virgin. He lived for over thirty-three years as a human like us. He lived among our pain and suffering. He saw it up close and personal. He heard our cries. He saw and spoke with people suffering under the curse of sin—people born blind, lame, deaf, or mute; people under the control of demonic forces; people dying before their time; people suffering oppression under evil men; and people devoid of hope.

Jesus saw and lived among all this and more. Yet amid the chaos of sin, He brought hope. He brought order to chaos and healing to the sick. He fed the hungry and lifted the oppressed. He brought peace to those hurting. And then, He gave His life on the cross, paying the debt for our sins. He died for us. He brought us victory over the curse and penalty of sin.

Because of His earthly ministry, His death on the cross, and His resurrection from the grave, there is coming a day when sin will be no more. Pain and sorrow will be no more. Death will be no more. He has won the victory! Although we suffer under the consequences of sin, there is coming a day when we will suffer no more. We don't know when, but we can count on it happening.

When John was given his revelation, he wrote near the end in Revelation 21:3–5, "And I heard a loud voice from the throne saying, 'Behold, the dwelling place of God is with man. He will dwell with them, and they will be his people, and God himself will be with them as their God. He will wipe away every tear from their eyes, and death shall be no more, neither shall there be mourning, nor crying, nor pain anymore, for the former things have passed away.' And he who was seated on the throne said, 'Behold, I am making all things new.' Also he said, 'Write this down, for these words are trustworthy and true.'"

May you find peace and hope, knowing the end of the story. It is not just a story written in the Bible. It is our story. We are part of it. And it will come to pass as it has been written.

Trials Are a Normal Part of Life

Although pain and suffering are not part of God's original plan for humankind, they are now a part of life here in this world. Therefore, as we contemplate the question of *why me, Lord*, we need to come to grips with the fact that hard times are now a normal part of life. None of us will escape this life unscathed, unscarred, or unhurt by the trials we face.

Job was a man who went through tremendous tragedy in his life. He lost virtually everything! After losing his family, his wealth, and even his own health, some of his friends came to counsel him. Job's reply is lengthy, but of note is what he says in Job 14:1. Job says, "Man who is born of a woman is few of days and full of trouble." The word *trouble* in this verse is used only seven times in the Old Testament, five of those in the book of Job. The primary meaning of the word is "a state of agitation or uproar." As used by Job in this verse, it denotes "the chaos of ordinary life in this world." He is saying that chaos, or hard times, is normal in this life!

Peter writes of this in 1 Peter 4:12, "Beloved, do not be surprised at the fiery trial when it comes upon you to test you, as though something strange were happening to you." Notice that he says it is not a matter of *if* but *when* we face fiery trials. The phrase *fiery trials* is one word in the Greek language, which literally means *the act or condition of being on fire or burning.* Figuratively, as Peter uses the word, it means a *fiery trial, calamity, or suffering.* Peter says, "Do not be shocked. Do not be surprised. You *will* experience some fiery trials in your life!"

I once heard an old preacher say, "You are coming out of a trial, in a trial, or heading into a trial!" I have also heard it said this way, "The forecast for life is … Trouble today, trials next week with a period of relief in between!" Hard times are part and parcel of this life. We cannot escape them. Nor should we harden our hearts so they will not hurt us as badly when they come. But we can prepare our hearts and minds for the trials we will face. This book will help you be prepared for the trials of your life.

Not All Trials Are Equal

When I speak of trials, tribulations, hardships, afflictions, and difficulties, I use these terms interchangeably. They all mean the same thing. However, that is not to say that each instance of such in our lives is the same.

Some of your trials will be life-altering. The tragic death of a close loved one or the diagnosis of a fatal illness can change your life and the lives of those around you in lasting ways. I had a motorcycle accident in 1994 when I hit some sand and went off the road. My right arm was broken, and I had other injuries that required several stitches. I was down for a few weeks until my arm healed, but now the only reminders of that accident are my memories of it and a scar on my chin. In 2007, when my son nearly died in a motorcycle accident, our lives were altered dramatically and forever.

I have experienced the loss of many loved ones. Most of those losses did not change the course of my life. But when my brother and his wife were murdered, our lives were forever changed. The point is that some trials are a bump on the path of life while others dramatically alter your life. The pain may eventually fade, but it never goes away completely. The scars remain, thinking can be altered, and you may find yourself waiting for the next shoe to drop.

Some trials are not much more than a nuisance. They hit you and cause only a slight deviation from the normal course of life before they are over. But sometimes, even these *little* trials can become huge and life-changing. You may experience less severe trials that pile on to the point that they seem much more severe. Do not just brush these off. The long-term stress of dealing with a series of *little* trials can affect physical, emotional, mental, and spiritual health.

Our Response to Trials Is Not Equal

Trials of varying degrees of severity will come your way. It is also important to keep in mind that the severity of our trials is very personal. Your personality, prior experience, and your physical/spiritual maturity level will change how the trials you face affect you. What may crush another person may bounce off you with little or no permanent pain. Do not allow such comparison to make your situation even worse.

Certainly, you may see qualities and strength in another person whom you wish to emulate or learn from, but know that this other person is *not you!* Do not look down on yourself because another person seems to ride above the storm and you seem to be crushed by the same storm. Trials, tribulations, hardships, and sufferings are very personal and will affect each person differently. Learn from others. Learn from your own trials. Learn from God's Word. You will grow and your own response to trials will change over time.

Sufferings and Trials Are Always Bearable

In the months following the tragedy of my brother's murder, I often felt completely crushed by the ordeal. Though others may have seen me as a strong Christian who was an example to follow, I did not feel that way. I felt that if one more feather was laid on my back, I would collapse from the weight. We each feel that way from time to time in the darkest and stormiest times of our lives.

But take heart. I believe that every trial we may find ourselves in is bearable. In 1 Corinthians 10:13, Paul writes, "No temptation has overtaken you that is not common to man. God is faithful, and he will not let you be tempted beyond your ability, but with the temptation, he will also provide the way of escape, that you may endure it." Many have probably heard this verse used regarding overcoming sin. The context of the verse, at first glance, may appeal to such an interpretation, and many scholars take this view exclusively. However, I believe there is an application of the verse we often miss.

The Greek word *peirasmos* translated as *temptation* is used some twenty-one times in the New Testament. In some contexts, it is clearly used to denote a temptation to sin. Luke uses the word in his Gospel account more than any other New Testament author (six times), so let us look at how he uses it in various ways. In Luke 4:13, the devil "ended every temptation [peirasmos]" of Jesus. The devil was tempting Jesus to sin. In Luke 8, in the parable of the seeds and the soil, we read that "they believe for a while, and in time of *testing* fall away" (Luke 8:13). Here he seems to say that when the going became rough, that is trials and hardships came, these people fell away from the faith.

In Luke's account of the Lord's prayer, he writes, as Matthew does, "And lead us not into temptation." (Luke 11:4) This seems to be a prayer for God to protect us from temptation to sin. In Jesus's last hours with His disciples, Jesus uses *peirasmos* when He is speaking to the disciples in the upper room. He says, "You are those who have stayed with me in my trials" (Luke 22:28). Here the word speaks of the difficulties Jesus faced in ministry. Then just a few verses later while in the garden, Jesus urges Peter, James, and John to "pray that you may not enter into temptation" (Luke 22:40). Here He seems to be speaking of temptation to sin through a lack of awareness.

The point is obvious that *peirasmos* is used in a couple of ways in the New Testament. The next word we should look at in 1 Corinthians 10:13 that helps with understanding this verse is the word *endure*. This word *hypopherō* means "to bear up" and is used only three times in the New Testament. Besides here, it is used in 2 Timothy 3:11, where Paul writes of the *persecutions* he *endured*. Peter uses the word in 1 Peter 2:19, where he writes about "enduring sorrows while suffering unjustly." In both instances, *hypopherō* is clearly connected to suffering brought on by persecution, which caused great difficulty.

It makes sense then to apply the same meaning of this word in 1 Corinthians 10:13. We are never told to *bear up under* the temptation to sin. We are told to flee such temptation. However, we should and can bear up under the trials, tribulations, afflictions, and hard times that come our way. I believe this is the promise of this verse. In every trial we face, God provides a way of escape for us. Note that the way of escape is not delivering us out of the trial but providing the means of enduring the trial through to the end. God makes a way for us to walk through our hard times. Sufferings and trials are always bearable!

It Is Not Wrong to Ask Why

"The one question you should never ask God is why. It is not for you to know why." After I became a follower of Jesus at 17 years old, I often heard phrases like this one. You may have heard similar teachings throughout your life. It might have been worded in different ways, but the idea was that we were simply to believe God and not question Him about why something was happening to us. It was as if to ask "Why" was to accuse God of *doing* something to us. Yet in almost every trial I have faced, the "Why" question just came out. It seemed a natural response to my circumstances. Yet, because of the teaching I had heard, every time I asked "Why", I felt guilty. I felt like a sub-par Christian.

During the aftermath of the murder of my brother and his wife, I often called out to God, "Why me?" As I searched the Bible for answers, I realized this teaching of not asking God *why* was bad theology. I discovered this while reading through the psalms for comfort.

Repeatedly in the book of Psalms, the writer asks God *why*. At least fifteen times in nine verses, he asks, "Why?" Before continuing to read this book, I encourage you to read the following psalms: Psalm 10:1, Psalm 22:1, Psalm 42:9, Psalm 43:2, Psalm 44:23–24, Psalm 74:1, Psalm 74:11, and Psalm 88:14. In each of these passages, the author of the psalms is clearly hurting. He is going through some tremendous trial or tribulation. And amid his pain and suffering, he asks God, "Why?"

Pain and suffering often blind us to what God is doing. It is true of us. It was true of David. And it was true of the other psalmists. We sometimes cannot see God at work. Because we cannot see God at work, we wonder if God has rejected us. The psalmist often wondered if God had forgotten him or was hiding His face from him. In Psalm 44:23, he even asks, "Why are you sleeping, O Lord?" In his humanity, in the middle of his sufferings and trials, he naturally wanted to know why he was going through such hard times. He wanted to know, "Why me?"

Considering the concept of asking God why, there are a couple of important observations we should make. First, nowhere in the Bible can I find a case of God condemning David or anyone else for asking why. In fact, God quite obviously tells us to pray. There are many facets of prayer, but part of it is pouring out our soul before God. Read Psalm 88 as a great example of someone pouring out his soul before God. In prayer, we should pour out our anguish, our pain, our confusion, and our questions. God sees deep into our hearts already. He knows our anguish. He knows our pain. He knows our confusion. He knows our questions. He knows our hearts better than we know our own hearts.

Since God can see deep into our hearts, why not simply be honest with Him about the pain we are feeling? By doing so, we are humbly admitting to God our weakness and inability to understand our situation or to hold up under the pressure we are experiencing. Isn't this exactly where God wants us? He wants us humble before Him, so do not hesitate to ask why. Let it out. Be honest. Be humble.

Another observation worth looking at is that in nearly every passage where David or another psalmist asks why, he also declares his faith in God in the same psalm. He does not doubt God's power and ability to deliver. He asks why but knows that God can deliver him. In his anguish and pain, he finds God still worthy of praise and worship. It is as if the pain of trials and sufferings pointed the psalmists to God, which is a very important topic we will delve deeply into later in this book.

One last thought about asking God why. It is a rhetorical question on our part. It is not likely that we will hear some booming voice give us an answer to our question. We may not even hear a still small voice whispering the answer to us. We should not let this lack of specificity turn us from our faith in God. While He may not give us the answers we seek, He will most definitely comfort us in our suffering. He has and always will walk with us through our difficult situations.

We may never know an exact answer to why, but that does not mean there are no answers. The Bible answers this important question for us. In the rest of this book, I will share with you the answers God gave me when I was deep in the pain and confusion of my darkest times.

Part 2

What Causes Our Suffering?

Introduction to Part 2

When we think about why we endure sufferings, trials, tribulations, afflictions, and hardships, we are really asking three separate questions. We are certainly asking, "Why is this happening to me?" This is a specific question that requires a specific answer that we may never receive from God. But there are two additional questions we are asking at the same time for which the Bible gives us answers.

When asking, "Why me?", we are also asking, "What is causing my suffering?" and "What is the purpose of my suffering?" If we want to know *why me*, we must seek answers for each of these corollary questions. In part 2, we will examine the causes of our suffering.

Chapter 2

Our Suffering May Be Caused by Our Own Sinfulness and Foolishness

There is only one man in all human history who can claim to have never sinned or acted foolishly. Of course, that man is Jesus Christ. For the rest of us, we will deal with our own sinful behavior and folly while we are living this earthly life. We make poor decisions. We willfully sin. Occasionally, we may be blindsided by temptation and fall into sin. We act foolishly. All of which leads to consequences that may bring about suffering in our lives.

This is called the *law of sowing and reaping*. My wife and I, have over the years, dabbled in growing vegetable gardens. I say dabbled because although we start them, we rarely find the time to keep up with the cultivating of the soil and pruning of the plants, so our yield is usually very small. But even in my limited knowledge of gardening, I know for a fact that when we plant corn seeds, if anything grows, it will be corn. It is the same with green beans, tomatoes, cucumbers, and squash.

The *law of sowing and reaping* is a foundational law in both the physical world and the spiritual world. When God created the heavens and the earth in Genesis 1–2, He set this law in motion. Genesis 1:11–12 states, "Let the earth sprout vegetation, plants yielding seed, and fruit trees bearing fruit in which is their seed, each according to its kind, on the earth. And it was so. The earth brought forth vegetation, plants yielding seed according to their own kinds, and trees bearing fruit in which is their seed, each according to its kind. And God saw that it was good." Thus, the law of sowing and reaping began.

No one can escape this law of life. It may seem that some people get by with few or no consequences for their sinful behavior. It may seem this way to someone looking on from the outside but know that each person will reap what he sows.

I spent over twenty years working for the Federal Bureau of Prisons as a correctional officer. Some would say prison guard, but we like our more elite-sounding title of correctional officer. I worked in two different prisons during my career. I started and ended my career at the US Medical Center for Federal Prisoners in Springfield, Missouri. In the middle of my career, I worked for five years at the Supermax or ADX in Florence, Colorado. Both prisons were filled with men who were reaping the consequences of the criminal behavior they planted.

I heard inmates claim their innocence more times than I could count, and I could have been a rich man had I been given a dollar each time. Still, there were a few inmates during my career who admitted that they were justly doing time for the crimes they committed. It was refreshing to hear a hardened criminal admit to being at fault.

While the inmates I worked with over the years may have been suffering more extreme consequences for their behavior, all of us will reap the consequences of sinful or foolish behavior. Such was my case the first and only time I have ever been fired from a job.

In 1981, my wife and I moved from Virginia to Colorado. Shortly thereafter, I took a job with Wendy's as a manager. It did not take long until they promoted me to head manager of my store. I was quite successful. My store was normally in the top 5 in the Denver Metro area of twenty-five Wendy's corporate stores. In 1984, we decided to move back to Virginia. Because of my experience and success with Wendy's International in Denver, I was hired as a manager with a much smaller Wendy's franchise in Martinsville, Virginia.

It started off smoothly enough. I was good at my job and I knew I was good at my job. In fact, I was so good that I changed procedures and practices that had been in place for quite some time in this smaller franchise. My supervisor would come in and correct what I had done, telling me to do it their way. "Who did this guy think he was telling me to change how I was running my restaurant?" I listened, nodded, and told him I would comply. Then as soon as he left, I completely rejected his admonition and went back to my way.

This went on for a few months. Finally, my supervisor had enough of my belligerence and pride. He came in one day, set me down in the dining room, and fired me! He fired me! Impossible! Unbelievable! I was the best thing that had happened to this Podunk small-time franchise! I was Wally Long, restaurant manager extraordinaire. They could have learned a great deal from me, but they blew it by firing me instead.

Instead of sowing humility, patience, and hard work, I planted pride, impatience, and stubbornness. What grew from my planting was financial hardship. I had a small baby girl, a wife, a house, and the resulting bills but no income. This could not have happened at a worse time. I found a low-paying job at a textile factory in Martinsville, but the pay was low, and I became just one of many low-income workers trying to make ends meet. Fortunately, God taught me some valuable lessons through my foolish behavior. I would like to say that I learned them once and was done. But alas, I am sometimes slow to learn and have had to learn the same lessons many times throughout my adult life.

I could go on telling self-deprecating stories, but I will not bore you with such details, and I would like to keep some of my dignity intact. Besides, you probably know exactly what I am talking about. You may have been there and done that. None of us is immune to the law of sowing and reaping.

Job suffered as few in this life have ever suffered. In Job 1, he lost his servants, his livestock, and all his children. Then in chapter 2, his health was attacked. Shortly thereafter, three friends came to be with Job in his despair. In chapter 4, one of his friends Eliphaz the Temanite tried to help Job with his *wise counsel*. He says in Job 4:8, "As I have seen, those who plow iniquity and sow trouble reap the same." Whether or not his counsel was sincere or applicable in Job's case, it was certainly true. "Those who sow iniquity will reap iniquity. Those who sow trouble will reap trouble."

Paul wrote of this universal law as well. Galatians 6:7 (ESV) says, "Do not be deceived: God is not mocked, for whatever one sows, that will he also reap." It would be great if we could skirt this law or if we could bypass the effects of it. However, as we all know from experience, this cannot be done. In Luke 15, the prodigal son thought he could escape this law. He, in his desire to live the *good life*, demanded the inheritance owed him from his father. The father granted his request. The son went out and *sowed his wild oats*. Before long, he had spent all he had and found himself living in a pigpen, "longing to be fed with the pods that the pigs ate, and no one gave him anything" (Luke 15:16).

Sometimes we suffer tribulation and hardship because of our sinful behavior, unwise decisions, and pride. We might suffer financial hardship due to unwise financial decisions. We might lose a job because of our pride. We might live the wild life and contract an incurable disease. We might ruin relationships with words spoken rashly.

Sometimes the consequences we reap will be not much more than a minor nuisance. We fix the issue, make right the wrong, and move on. Sometimes, the consequences we reap will have long-lasting effects. It may take years to rebuild what has been broken or make right what has fallen apart.

What should we do when we find ourselves amid trials, tribulations, and sufferings that we have caused by our own sinfulness, pride, and foolishness? We cannot just continue as if nothing had happened and hope it will all go away. We must be humble enough to admit we blew it, confess it to the Lord, and seek His forgiveness. Proverbs 28:13 says, "Whoever conceals his transgressions will not prosper, but he who confesses and forsakes them will obtain mercy."

In addition to confessing our sinful behavior and seeking forgiveness, we should seek to learn what we can from our mistakes so that we can avoid doing the same in the future. A very wise man once wrote, "The prudent sees danger and hides himself, but the simple go on and suffer for it" (Proverbs 22:3). If we seek to learn from our mistakes, we may avoid future danger rather than walking headlong into more trouble.

We may also need to invest much time in repairing broken relationships in our families, among our friends, and with coworkers. It will be a humbling experience to admit to others that you were wrong and ask for their forgiveness. They may not take it well. You may not save your job. But the only way to move past the trouble you put yourself into is to attempt to make right what you have done wrong. You may be unable to do so in every circumstance, but you should try.

Chapter 3

Our Suffering May Be Caused by the Sin of Others

Sometimes the troubles we face are caused by the sins of others. You may have done nothing wrong, but because of the evil or careless actions of other people, you could find yourself enduring hardship and suffering. One need not read or see much news to read and see that this world is a place of much suffering and pain. Murder, human trafficking, child abuse, and riots seem to be common items in the news. Evil in this world is on full display in every news broadcast and newspaper story. We see it regularly on our TV shows and movies. *People do bad things.*

When people do bad things, someone suffers. Usually, many people suffer because of the actions of one person or group of people. It is much like the dropping of a stone in a still pond. The effects of that dropped stone continue for a comparatively long time, spreading ever farther outward from the beginning of the ripples. Every crime and every act of evil affects many people and brings about much suffering.

In Genesis 37–50, we read one of the most fascinating stories of God's providence in the Bible. Joseph, the son of Jacob with Rachel, was a decent seventeen-year-old kid. The Bible records no wrongs or sins of Joseph. We know he must have sinned, but the writers record none of them. Yet Joseph suffered through the ungodly and evil actions of other people. As a youth, Joseph may not have been as wise as he could have been. In Genesis 37, we read he tattled on his brothers. He was favored by his father and given a very nice robe. He then had a couple of dreams about which he told his family. Joseph interpreted both dreams to mean that his family, including his father, mother, and brothers, would one day bow down to him. I wonder about the wisdom of sharing such dreams with his family the way he did. Genesis 37:11 states, "And his brothers were jealous of him, but his father kept the saying in mind."

His brothers sold him to a slave trader who then sold him to Potiphar, the captain of the guards of the Pharaoh in Egypt. Joseph worked hard, was blessed by God, and found favor with Potiphar, in so much that Potiphar made Joseph the overseer of his estate. But Potiphar's wife, apparently very attracted to Joseph, tried to seduce Joseph. This went on for some time until she grabbed Joseph, who fled, leaving his garment in her hands. She accused him of trying to rape her, so Potiphar had Joseph thrown into prison.

Joseph spent over two years in prison for a crime he did not commit. While there, he interpreted the dreams of a couple of Pharaoh's servants, who had been sentenced to prison as well. Through a series of God-ordained circumstances, Joseph ends up before the Pharaoh to interpret the Pharaoh's troubling dreams. Joseph soon finds himself in charge of the entire kingdom, answering only to the Pharaoh. In his position, he later saves the lives of his entire family when the country is in a terrible drought. His boyhood dreams had come true after all. His brothers had bowed down to him. After he revealed himself to his brothers, he said this to them in Genesis 50:20, "As for you, you meant evil against me, but God meant it for good, to bring it about that many people should be kept alive, as they are today."

Joseph had done nothing wrong, only that he could have used some discretion and wisdom before sharing his dreams with the family. Yet he suffered at the hands of others. He suffered because of their sins. We will look further at Joseph's story in chapter 13.

Our family suffered due to the evil actions of a twelve-year-old boy. To this day, we have no solid reason why he chose on that fateful evening to pick up a pistol intending to kill his father, mother, brother, and sister. But that one evening and his decision to do evil drastically affected the lives of many people. He caused great suffering in the lives of all connected. My brother's family and our family suffered. The church they had attended suffered. The detective and police officers who showed up at the scene of the crime suffered. One detective told me years later that he still had nightmares stemming from that event.

People do bad things, and other people suffer. What are we to do when we suffer because of the sins of other people? Our normal human response after the pain caused us is to be angry at the offending person. We may find ourselves wanting revenge or hating that person. We might, whether consciously or unconsciously, ask God to bring that person to harm. We might ask God to get our revenge for us.

This may be our normal human response, but it is not a beneficial response. When we begin to hate and seek revenge, we only perpetuate the evil that was done to us. We give it fuel to continue to wreak havoc on the lives of innocent people. We give place to hatred, anger, and bitterness, which become in us a form of spiritual bondage. Often, we cannot control our immediate emotional response to the harm done to us by another. We respond with anger, hurt, hatred, or some such negative emotion. But we can choose, after the initial emotion, to respond in a biblical manner.

When we are hurt by the sins of other people and we suffer trials and hardships in the aftermath of their sins, we must, at some point along the way, choose to respond correctly. In fact, there are several choices we must consciously make.

1. *We must choose to forgive.*

Jesus, in the prayer He taught His disciples, said in Matthew 6:12, "And forgive us our debts, as we also have forgiven our debtors." He is teaching them that forgiveness is a crucial part of the Christian life. Forgiveness is the releasing of a debt owed, whether real or perceived. When someone wrongs us, we feel they owe us a *debt*. In forgiveness, we release them from that obligation.

The writer of Hebrews, in Hebrews 8:12, quotes Isaiah 43:25, "For I will be merciful toward their iniquities, and I will remember their sins no more." I do not think God literally forgets anything. That would violate His divine trait of omniscience. When He says, "I will remember their sins no more," He is saying that He releases the debt owed for our sins. He removes it from the debit column. Of course, we know Jesus paid the debt on the cross, giving God the chance to *forget/forgive* our debt.

If, as humans, we choose to hold on to the debt, we are holding on to the pain as well. We are providing fertile soil in which anger, hatred, and bitterness can grow in our hearts. We are binding ourselves to the wrong that was done to us. This is no way to live. Holding on to this perceived debt will not hurt the offender. It will hurt you and by extension, the relationships you have with those close to you. It has been said that "unforgiveness is like drinking poison and hoping the person who hurt us gets sick." Unfortunately, if you hold on to the anger and bitterness, you are the one being affected by it. You allow the wrong of another to continue to poison your life.

2.   *We must choose to continue moving toward forgiveness.*

The forgiveness you seek toward a person who has hurt you may take time. It will probably be an ongoing process. I found this to be true in the aftermath of the tragedy that hit us on March 1, 2011.

On March 5, 2011, only four days after the tragedy, I began to get a strong sense, deep in my soul, that I needed to visit my nephew who, just days before, had murdered his father and mother and almost killed his little brother and sister. It was a feeling I could not explain. I was hurting. I was emotionally distraught. I was angry. But I knew in my heart God wanted me to go visit him. I spoke with my family. They did not understand it either. My dear wife Sylvia, not understanding but trusting God, decided to go with me. I made the arrangements. Then on March 7, 2011, we headed to the prison for the visit.

We arrived at the facility and went through visitor processing. Then they ushered us into a small room with a stainless-steel table in the middle of it. We were seated on one side of the table with my nephew and his guardian ad litem on the other side. It is difficult to describe the emotions I felt while looking at the boy who had, just days before, murdered my brother: confusion, grief, sadness, and pity. Other emotions fought to come to the surface: anger, rage, hatred, and revenge.

As we sat there making small talk, Sylvia and I sobbing most of the time, I experienced an inner struggle like I had never experienced before or since. I wanted to hate him. I wanted to be angry with him. I wanted him to pay for what he had done. I was at a defining crossroads in my life. Down one road, there was peace, love, and forgiveness. Down the other road, there was anger, hatred, and bitterness. When the visit was at an end, I stood up, reached across that table, and hugged my nephew. I told him I was his uncle and that I still cared for him. I honestly could not get the word love out of my mouth, but I think it was communicated. To say this was difficult for me is a tremendous understatement.

I do not know if my simple hug had any effect or impact on my nephew. It did not seem to. He showed no emotion. I can only pray that one day he remembers that act of love and kindness. I pray that when he remembers it, he is led to a place of repentance, confession, and healing.

I believe with all my heart that had I not taken the simple step of hugging my nephew and showing him some kindness, life for me and my family would not be what it is today. Anger, hatred, and bitterness could have easily consumed me for many years, affecting my life dramatically. I was not at the place of forgiveness toward him yet, but it was the first small step that led me to be able to truly forgive him several months later. I was unable to tell him face-to-face since he refused further meetings with me, but I was able to tell him in a crowded courtroom during a hearing several years into his seven-year sentence. I felt great joy and happiness to testify to the courtroom, and to my nephew, that I had forgiven him. I had released the debt for the pain his evil actions had caused my family.

Forgiveness is the responsibility of every person, regardless of the extent of the pain caused by another. By not forgiving, we harbor the pain and allow it to bind us. We build a wall of anger, hatred, and bitterness around our hearts toward the person who hurt us, that will affect every area of our lives. We think to ourselves that he/she does not deserve our forgiveness. That may be true, but then we do not deserve the forgiveness God so freely offers.

You may be suffering trials and tribulations because of the sins of other people. Do not allow that wrong to control your life. Seek the grace God gives to forgive that person.

3.   *We must choose to pray for the offender.*

In Mark 11, Jesus teaches His disciples about faith and prayer. He says in Mark 11:22–25, "Have faith in God. Truly, I say to you, whoever says to this mountain, 'Be taken up and thrown into the sea,' and does not doubt in his heart, but believes that what he says will come to pass, it will be done for him. Therefore, I tell you, whatever you ask in prayer, believe that you have received it, and it will be yours. And whenever you stand praying, forgive, if you have anything against anyone, so that your Father also who is in heaven may forgive you your trespasses."

I want you to notice how He ends this teaching on faith and prayer. He says, "Forgive those with whom you have a problem." When someone hurts you, you will have something against them. You have a perceived debt that they owe you. Jesus says to forgive them while you are in prayer. The next logical step is to pray for that person. I have found that I cannot hate someone and pray for them at the same time.

I worked at the Supermax federal prison from 1995 to 2000. We housed the worst of the worst in the federal prison system. Every inmate there was a killer, terrorist, major gang leader, or had done some other heinous crime while in a federal prison. In my housing unit, I had Ted Kaczynski, Tim McVeigh, Ramzi Yousef (1993 Trade Center bomber), and many other inmates, much worse than these but not as famous. These men were easy to hate. It is an understatement to say it was a very dark place.

After a few years of working there, the darkness was affecting my life outside of the prison. I was more angry, short with my family, and lacked any semblance of joy in my life. Finally, at my wit's end, I cried out to God, "I need help! I don't know how to fix this!" Deep in my heart, I seemed to hear this whisper, "Pray for the inmates at your job." What? I did not like that answer, so I asked again, and the same answer came back to my heart. I fought with God for several days but the idea just grew in my heart until it was screaming at me, "Pray for the inmates!" "OK! I give up! I will pray for them."

I began a practice of praying for each inmate in my housing unit at the beginning of each shift. Normally, it was a simple one- or two-sentence prayer. Not long after beginning this practice, I noticed a few changes. My attitude began to change, both at work and at home. The hate and anger were gone. I found joy in my life outside of work. And then I noticed that my interactions with the inmates were changing as well. They were more cooperative with me. In fact, I could often get them to cooperate when others could not. I learned a great lesson. You cannot hate someone and pray for them at the same time. So pray for the one who hurt you.

4. *We must choose to love.*

Paul wrote in Colossians 3:12–15, "Put on then, as God's chosen ones, holy and beloved, compassionate hearts, kindness, humility, meekness, and patience, bearing with one another and, if one has a complaint against another, forgiving each other; as the Lord has forgiven you, so you also must forgive. And above all these put on love, which binds everything together in perfect harmony. And let the peace of Christ rule in your hearts, to which indeed you were called in one body. And be thankful."

"Above all, put on love!" The word for *put on* in verse 12 means to *clothe with.* We are to clothe ourselves in love. We wrap love around our hearts and minds like we would wrap ourselves in a nice garment. The clothing we wear becomes what people first see when they look at us. It becomes part of a description someone might use to pick us out in a crowd. It is the same with love. When we clothe ourselves with love, people see love in us. It becomes a prominent descriptor. It defines us.

Love is often difficult. Anyone who has been married for any length of time can tell you that the feeling of love is not always there. That is because love is not a feeling. It is a choice. I choose to love my wife when she is hard to love (which is not often!). My wife chooses to love me when I am hard to love (which is much more often!). Love is a choice. We must choose to love those who hurt us deeply. That does not mean we must allow them to be a regular part of our lives, especially if they are toxic in their ways. We may need to love them from a distance, but we *must* love them!

Chapter 4

Our Suffering May Be Caused by the Enemy

At the beginning of chapter 1, we looked at the initial cause of pain and suffering in the world. Sin entered the universe when Satan rebelled against God. Then sin entered God's perfectly created world when Adam and Eve followed Satan's suggestion to eat the forbidden fruit. Adam and Eve's disobedience of God's command set in motion the reign of chaos, pain, and suffering that has only gotten worse through the millennia. Satan, through his lies, deceived Adam and Eve, destroying the perfect communion they had with their Creator. Now instead of peace and perfect harmony, they would experience guilt, sorrow, and grief.

Satan continues this campaign of terror and destruction today. Peter writes in 1 Peter 5:8, "Be sober-minded; be watchful. Your adversary the devil prowls around like a roaring lion, seeking someone to devour." The devil is looking to devour you and me. He wants to make us ineffectual in our walk as followers of Jesus Christ. One of his methods of attack is through hardship and suffering. Through tragedy, he will try to cause us to lose faith in God Almighty. He will try to embitter us. He will try to take away our joy. The trials he throws into our path will test our faith.

This happened to Job. Job was a godly man. "There was a man in the land of Uz whose name was Job, and that man was blameless and upright, one who feared God and turned away from evil" (Job 1:1). He had many sons and daughters and a huge estate. He was a wealthy man by any standard you might use to measure. Satan, wishing to show God that Job only worshipped him because of the great blessings God bestowed on Job, came to God and challenged God to a duel of sorts. He told God that if Job lost all he had, he would curse God. God, confident in Job's sincere faith, accepted the challenge.

God granted Satan permission to destroy all that Job owned. In short order, his servants, his livestock, and then all his children were gone. Job did not curse God. Then Satan was allowed to bring physical illness to Job. He ended up covered "with loathsome sores from the sole of his foot to the crown of his head" (Job 2:7). Still Job held on to his faith in God. Job was suffering greatly. An attack of Satan in his life caused his afflictions.

Satan was the direct cause of Job's hardships. This may seem hard for us to contemplate. Satan attacked Job but did so with the permission of God. Why did God allow such pain in Job's life? None of us can come close to knowing the mind of God is such a matter. But God had a plan and God was glorified in Job's life. He then blessed Job with much more than he had lost. And we have the testimony of Job to encourage us throughout the ages.

Paul understood this idea of suffering at the hand of Satan. He writes in 2 Corinthians 12:7, "So to keep me from becoming conceited because of the surpassing greatness of the revelations, a thorn was given me in the flesh, a messenger of Satan to harass me, to keep me from becoming conceited." We do not know what this "thorn in the flesh" was, but Paul directly attributed it to the harassment of Satan. He suffered at the hands of the enemy of God. Satan was trying to knock Job off course in his walk with God.

Through the years in my time as a US Marine and as a civilian, I had much training in land navigation. I learned how to read a topographical map, orient the map, use a compass, and find my way through difficult terrain. Often, we would find ourselves navigating through terrain that was very dense, making it impossible to travel in a straight line. In such situations, they taught us to find a landmark in the same direction as our destination and move toward that landmark. When we arrived at that landmark, we would ensure that our orientation was correct, find another landmark, and continue the journey.

While moving toward a landmark, it was very important to keep our focus on the landmark. If our attention deviated from that landmark, it would be easy to lose our way, for even the slightest deviation could cause us to lose sight of the landmark. This is one of Satan's strategies for trials and tribulations. He wishes to cause us to deviate from the path God has for us to walk. He wants us out in the weeds, thorns, and brambles of life. He wants us to stray so far off the path of travel that we find ourselves lost in our pain and suffering. He wants us to be ineffective in our Christian life. He wants to make us feel defeated.

In the well-known chapter of faith, Hebrews 11, we read a who's who list of men and women who had great faith in God. If you were to read the stories of the great people of faith, you would read much of the trials, tribulations, and hardships they walked through. These men and women accomplished great deeds through faith. They walked through great trials by faith. They saw much victory because of their faith.

Yet when we reach the end of the chapter, we read of others who did not fare so well on their journey. Hebrews 11:35–38 states, "Some were tortured, refusing to accept release, so that they might rise again to a better life. Others suffered mocking and flogging, and even chains and imprisonment. They were stoned, they were sawn in two, they were killed with the sword. They went about in skins of sheep and goats, destitute, afflicted, mistreated—of whom the world was not worthy—wandering about in deserts and mountains, and in dens and caves of the earth." The writer of the book of Hebrews does not record the names of these great people for us, but their faith lives on. They suffered at the hands of the enemy because of their faith. Yet they never lost their faith. Regardless of the outcome of the trials we face through the evil actions of our enemy, we must hold on to our faith in God Almighty.

We may never know if our trials and afflictions are directly caused by the enemy of God. Naming the cause of our suffering is not nearly as important as keeping our eyes focused on the landmarks that lead us in the right direction. There will be more on this in a later chapter. Just know that sometimes Satan may cause our sufferings and afflictions. Satan is at war with God and with all things godly. He is always looking for opportunities to harass God's people, intending to cause them to fall away from serving and loving God.

Chapter 5

Our Suffering May Be Caused by the Storms that Fall on Everyone

On the evening of May 22, 2011, an EF5 tornado struck Joplin, Missouri. This devastating tornado killed 158 people, with several thousand injured. It damaged nearly 8,000 buildings while destroying almost 4,000. The cost of this incident was over $2.8 billion.

In the aftermath of this natural disaster, there was much suffering. Christians and non-Christians alike suffered. People of all religions suffered. Good people and not-so-good people suffered. The destruction was no respecter of persons, religion, wealth, or status. It struck and struck hard, wreaking havoc in the lives of many thousands of people. We could say the same of the many earthquakes, tidal waves, tornadoes, floods, blizzards, wildfires, droughts, and other disasters that we read about in the news nearly every day. When they hit, they do much damage to anyone and anything caught in their swath of destruction.

Solomon writes of this in Ecclesiastes 9:2, "It is the same for all, since the same event happens to the righteous and the wicked, to the good and the evil, to the clean and the unclean, to him who sacrifices and him who does not sacrifice. As the good one is, so is the sinner, and he who swears is as he who shuns an oath." Jesus, teaching His disciples about loving enemies, makes an interesting statement in the middle of His teaching. He says in Matthew 5:45, "For he [God, the Father] makes his sun rise on the evil and on the good, and sends rain on the just and on the unjust." When it rains, we all get wet. When a drought comes, we all suffer the dryness. When a tornado goes on the rampage, it will destroy nearly everything in its path.

This does not mean we will automatically suffer death, damage, or destruction when we are struck by a storm that affects everyone. God sometimes intervenes to bring about miraculous protection and deliverance from such storms. We rarely, if ever, will understand why God delivers one but not another. He has His reasons and often He keeps those reasons to himself.

God intervened on behalf of our family on December 17, 2002. In October 2002, we moved into the home we had just purchased near Mount Vernon, Missouri. We spent weeks getting the house set up and boxes unpacked. On the evening of December 17, a major thunderstorm was brewing west and south of us. That storm spawned an EF1 tornado, which started in the creek bed a few hundred yards south of our house. We were the first place to be struck by this tornado. It destroyed our thirty-five-foot-by-seventy-foot barn. The flying debris from the destroyed barn knocked out windows and punched several holes in our roof. But our home remained standing and our family safe. Some of our neighbors did not fare so well.

Our closest neighbor was lying in her bed when the storm hit. It picked up her double-wide mobile home and dropped it several yards away. It caved in on her. She survived with hardly a scratch. After hitting us, the tornado traveled about a three-fourth mile across a field and destroyed several homes, killing one person. It then traveled across another field before doing terrible damage to several homes in a mobile home park before destroying another brick home and then dissipating.

Why save our home and not others? It was almost as if God had His hand on our home so that the storm would not tear it to the ground. Take the barn. Take the windows. But do not take the house. I cannot know exactly why God saved our house, but I know that our home has provided many blessings to others through the years since that storm hit. God had a plan for us and for our home. Since then, we have become a bit more prepared for storms.

We can and should do what we can to prepare for natural disasters. We can store food and water and build emergency shelters in our homes. We can have an emergency radio for communication in case the phone service goes out and install emergency generators for electrical service. We can do all of this and more but still lose nearly everything in a natural disaster. We can do nothing to prepare and come out nearly unscathed. Who knows why? Only God.

You may suffer because of some natural disaster. You may wonder why. Why didn't God save you? Why did God not protect you and your property? You may especially wonder about such thoughts when you see or hear of miraculous deliverance from other people in the same disaster. Do not be dismayed. The cause of your suffering is not nearly as important as the purpose of your suffering. Keep reading. There will be much more on the purpose of suffering in part 3.

Chapter 6

Our Suffering May Simply Be the Result of Living in a Fallen World

We started this book in chapter one with some thoughts about Adam and Eve and the fall of man through sin. Let us review it here. God created Adam and Eve in a perfect world. They had each other. They had the Garden of Eden to "work it and keep it" (Genesis 2:15). They had all the animals, none of which wanted to kill and eat them! Food was abundant from the trees and plants in the *garden*. They had continual glorious weather. Best of all, they had perfect communion with their Creator! Life was good! Life was perfect! They had it made in the shade!

Adam and Eve had everything they could want to make them happy and keep them content. God gave them only a few rules to live by. They were to fill the earth with more human beings through an act that also brought them great pleasure. They were to oversee the earth, along with the abundance of plant and animal life. They were to cultivate and work the land. These are all positive commands. Things they were to do. God gave them one command about what not to do. In Genesis 2:16–17, God said, "You may surely eat of every tree of the garden, but of the tree of the knowledge of good and evil you shall not eat, for in the day that you eat of it you shall surely die."

We all know what happened. Satan, in his attempt to thwart God's perfect world, tempted Adam and Eve to disobey God. They gave in to Satan's lies and ate from the tree of the knowledge of good and evil. They did the one and only thing God told them *not* to do! Sin had entered God's perfect creation.

When God confronted them, He told them how life for them would take some dramatic turns. To Eve, God said, "I will surely multiply your pain in childbearing; in pain you shall bring forth children. Your desire shall be for your husband, and he shall rule over you" (Genesis 3:16). I wonder if some measure of pain was originally part of God's childbirth plan because He says that He would "multiply her pain."

To Adam, God said, "Because you have listened to the voice of your wife and have eaten of the tree of which I commanded you, 'You shall not eat of it,' cursed is the ground because of you; in pain you shall eat of it all the days of your life; thorns and thistles it shall bring forth for you; and you shall eat the plants of the field. By the sweat of your face you shall eat bread, till you return to the ground, for out of it you were taken; for you are dust, and to dust you shall return" (Genesis 3:17–19).

Without getting into the science of this and into the weeds (pun intended) of this curse, the point is clear: life was about to get much more difficult for Adam and Eve. Childbirth would be harder. Growing food would be harder because of the thorns, thistles, and weeds. Killing for food would be harder because the animals would soon learn to fear man, even to the point of striking back and becoming the predators.

Sin and suffering had come into the world. The world was now a fallen world. Death had come where there was once only life. Chaos now reigned where there was once perfect order. Pain and suffering replaced the goodness of God's original creation. Now many millennia since that fateful day, sin has had thousands of years to reap its ugly consequences on mankind.

Everywhere we feel the effect of sin and the curse. The effect seems to grow exponentially. In my short sixty-three years of life, I can see the faster and faster advance of sin and the curse. Birth defects are more frequent. Starvation around the world is more prevalent, not less. Sickness abounds. War is continual. Corruption in nations, governments, businesses, and society is ever-increasing. Not a week goes by without someone in my small church asking for prayer for a friend or relative fighting cancer.

We indeed live in a fallen world, and we feel the effects of it all around us. It is par for the course in our lives. We will experience suffering through trials and hardships because of sin. Of course, Jesus came to break the *power of canceled sin* as Charles Wesley wrote in "O For a Thousand Tongues to Sing." We also know that because of the sacrifice of Jesus on the cross, there is coming a day when sin and the curse of sin will be no more. The whole of God's perfect creation will be redeemed. Paul wrote of this in Romans 8:19–21, "For the creation waits with eager longing for the revealing of the sons of God. For the creation was subjected to futility, not willingly, but because of him who subjected it, in hope that the creation itself will be set free from its bondage to corruption and obtain the freedom of the glory of the children of God." We long for that day, but until then, we will live in this fallen world and will suffer because of sin and the curse.

Part 3

The Purposes of Our Suffering

Introduction to Part 3

In this next part of the book, we will examine how God uses our suffering. We will look at *why me* as it regards the purpose of suffering. When looking at this question, we should be careful to not fall into one of two extremes. Some people look at God as passive in the tragedies we face which cause suffering and hardship. We will say things like "God allowed this to happen to me for ..." Or we might ask, "Why did God allow this to happen?"

In our human way of thinking, this puts God in the category of a lazy referee in a game wherein He sits back and lets the game play out, only intervening at certain times for reasons only He knows. Such thinking, again in our human way of thinking, may attribute a sense of impotence to God. Or if He is not impotent, it may appear as though God does not care about this world and our lives.

Often the detractors of Christianity use this same line of thinking and come to similar conclusions. They look at the chaos and suffering in this world and reason that God does not exist. If He exists, He either does not care about this world or He is powerless to intervene and do anything about the mess He created. We may not agree with these conclusions, but if we look at God as a passive God, our thinking lines up much with those who dislike or do not follow Christianity.

Another extreme we should avoid is looking at God as a powerful and angry being waiting for us to step out of line so He can unleash His wrath on us. This view looks at all our problems as the result of our own sins. God is spanking us with our hardship and affliction. In this way of thinking, God is vindictive and harsh. He is not a loving father. He is a harsh disciplinarian who cannot wait to punish His wayward children.

Neither of these views is biblical. Yet God uses our suffering. He gives purpose to our suffering. It is said of politicians that they will never let a national tragedy or a rival's scandal go to waste. They will always find a way to use it politically. Although we say this *tongue in cheek* about politicians, it is absolutely true of our Almighty God. Regardless of the cause of our suffering, God will always use our tragedy to bring some benefit to us and glorify Himself. As we shape our view of suffering according to biblical purposes for suffering, we get a clearer picture of who God is and how He works in our lives through our hardships.

In part 3, we will look at the purpose of suffering in our lives. We will examine how God uses our suffering for His glory and for our good. As we examine each of the reasons or purposes for our trials, tribulations, hardships, and sufferings, you may see yourself in some or all of them. God is not limited to one purpose for your difficulty and tragedy. He will not allow your suffering to go to waste. God is working in your life, and one or more of the purposes for suffering detailed in part 3 will help answer your question, "Why me, Lord?"

Chapter 7

God Uses Our Suffering to Show Himself Strong in Us

We, as human beings, are very independent. We like to do and accomplish tasks by ourselves. We hate to admit we need help. To say, "I can't" is a big taboo. This is likely because of the pride that is part of our human nature.

The problem is that in our pride and self-sufficiency, people do not clearly see God in our lives. And we rob ourselves of the blessing of watching God at work. God knows this conundrum we face and will often use our trials, afflictions, and suffering to bring us to a point of weakness so He can show himself strong in us.

Such was the case with the apostle Paul. Paul had pride? Say it isn't so! Paul describes the situation in 2 Corinthians 12:5–7, "On behalf of this man I will boast, but on my behalf I will not boast, except of my weaknesses—though if I should wish to boast, I would not be a fool, for I would be speaking the truth; but I refrain from it, so that no one may think more of me than he sees in me or hears from me. So to keep me from becoming conceited because of the surpassing greatness of the revelations, a thorn was given me in the flesh, a messenger of Satan to harass me, to keep me from becoming conceited." He is writing of himself in these verses. He is saying that he certainly has reason to boast because of what God has done through him in the past. God gave him a great revelation of doctrine for the church. Paul wrote much of the New Testament and through his writing, shaped much of our church doctrine.

Notice what Paul writes in verse 7, He was given a *thorn in the flesh*. He states this thorn in the flesh was a *messenger of Satan*. We do not know what this thorn in the flesh was. Some speculate it was a physical ailment. Perhaps it was a weak body or poor eyesight. Was he attacked by Satan with God's permission? This seems to be the case with Paul as it was with Job. The text says that this messenger of Satan harassed Paul. The word for *harassed* is also translated as *buffet*. It means to strike with a fist. Satan, apparently, was given permission by God to beat up Paul.

In our way of thinking, this may seem harsh. God allows Satan to beat up on Paul? I am not sure I like the idea that Satan may beat me up with God's permission. Paul struggled with the idea as well. He writes in 2 Corinthians 12:8 (ESV), "Three times I pleaded with the Lord about this, that it should leave me." "God, please take away this pain!" "God, I cannot take this anymore. Please make it stop!" "God, do you not love me? Do not let Satan attack me anymore!" Paul prayed three times before God answered him. Paul reported God's response to his prayer in 2 Corinthians 12:9, "My grace is sufficient for you, for my power is made perfect in weakness." Paul now understood what was really going on in his life and was not only content with his suffering but boasted about it. He writes, "Therefore I will boast all the more gladly of my weaknesses, so that the power of Christ may rest upon me. For the sake of Christ I am content with weaknesses, insults, hardships, persecutions, and calamities. For when I am weak, then I am strong."

Paul learned this principle, "God uses our sufferings, trials, afflictions, and hardships to show himself strong in us." The trials and tribulations we face bring us to a place of weakness.

As much as we might dislike being in such a place, it is a good place to be. It is a place where we and other people best see God at work in our lives.

A few weeks after the murder of my brother and his wife, Anastasiya Bolton, a reporter for a news agency in Denver, Colorado, asked to meet with me at a local restaurant. She told me she would not be writing a story about the tragedy. She only wished to get to know me a bit better and gain my trust for a possible follow-up story several months down the road. Her honesty was refreshing, so I agreed to the meeting. We had a great conversation. She was true to her word. She reported nothing about our conversation.

In late October 2011, Anastasiya reached out to me about coming to our home in Missouri to do the follow-up story we talked about earlier in the spring. She wanted to show the people of Colorado how well the two children were doing. She and her photographer spent two days with us, interviewing family members and doing videos of our family in daily activities. A week later, she wrote me with this message, "Thank you for allowing us into your home to get to know you and your family better. I am not a Christian, but your family blessed me." She went on to say, "I have never felt peace in a home like I did in your home."

The amazing thing about her statement was that I was not feeling such peace. Life was still chaotic. We had two traumatized children living in our home. We were homeschooling them, along with our two youngest sons, who were still living at home. The children attended two counseling sessions each week. I was trying to adjust to being retired. Our family life was a big mess that seemed to be crushing us. Yet Anastasiya felt peace in our home! Why? It was because during our time of weakness, God was showing Himself strong in us! Anastasiya felt peace because God was at work. She felt it and saw it.

Jesus taught this principle in John 9. He was walking along with His disciples when they passed by a man who had been born blind. His disciples asked, "Rabbi, who sinned, this man or his parents, that he was born blind?" (John 9:2). Jesus answered, "It was not that this man sinned, or his parents, but that the works of God might be displayed in him" (John 9:3). This man was certainly experiencing hardship. He was blind and had been so since his birth. Yet God had plans for his suffering.

Jesus healed the man. The Jewish religious leaders refused to believe the man had been born blind and could now see. These leaders challenged the man in John 9:24. They said, "Give glory to God. We know that this man [referring to Jesus] is a sinner." The man born blind stood up to the Jews and made this bold statement in John 9:32–33, "Never since the world began has it been heard that anyone opened the eyes of a man born blind. If this man were not from God, he could do nothing." God showed Himself strong in this man's life and the man became a follower of Jesus.

The light of God shines in the hearts of His followers. However, sometimes that light is hidden from the world because of the junk we accumulate as we walk through life. Jesus spoke of this in Matthew 5:14–16, "You are the light of the world. A city set on a hill cannot be hidden. Nor do people light a lamp and put it under a basket, but on a stand, and it gives light to all in the house. In the same way, let your light shine before others, so that they may see your good works and give glory to your Father who is in heaven." God may use our trials to remove the basket so our light will shine brightly in the world. He may use our trials to brush the junk off us. God gets you and me out of the way so that others will see Him in us.

God is the sculptor who sees a beautiful statue in a block of stone. Michelangelo is attributed to have said, "In every block of marble I see a statue as plain as though it stood before me, shaped and perfect in attitude and action. I have only to hew away the rough walls that imprison the lovely apparition to reveal it to the other eyes as mine see it." The sculptor sees the statue in the stone. But then he must reveal the statue so that others can see it.

If you were Michelangelo's block of stone and had feelings, you would not appreciate the pain caused by the chisel. However, when all the extra was chiseled off, you would appreciate the beauty that was revealed through the work of the chisel in the hands of the master sculptor. God is continually sculpting us. His chisel is at work removing that which keeps others from seeing the Creator of the universe in us. It may be painful, but there is glory and beauty inside, which will only be revealed as the extra stone is removed.

I know firsthand the despair you may feel while going through your storms. You feel weak, helpless, and totally inadequate to cope. I know it hurts. It is hard. But do not give up. Do not lose faith in our loving God. Regardless of what has caused your suffering, God wants to use it to show Himself strong in you. He wants others to see His work in and through you. God's answer to Paul is His answer to you as well, "My grace is sufficient for you, for my power is made perfect in weakness" (2 Corinthians 12:9). It may be difficult, but your response should be the same as Paul's, "Therefore I will boast even more gladly of my weaknesses, so that the power of Christ may rest upon me. For the sake of Christ I am content with weaknesses, insults, hardships, persecutions, and calamities. For when I am weak, then I am strong" (2 Corinthians 12:10).

Boast in your weakness. Be content in your weakness. Find purpose in your weakness. Find purpose in your trials and tribulations. Let go of your perceived control and allow God to show himself strong in you!

Chapter 8

God Uses Our Suffering to Strengthen Us

This principle may seem contradictory to the previous chapter, but it is not. In chapter 7, we discussed how God uses our weakness to show Himself strong in us. There are times, regardless of how strong we are spiritually or physically, that we become weakened by the trials we face. But much like an athlete causes pain to his own body in order to become stronger physically, our trials, though painful, cause us to grow stronger spiritually.

A dear friend of mine Lucinda, who lives in the town where I pastor a small Baptist Church, never expected something truly *bad* would happen to her. Lucinda began having consistent lower abdominal pain. After a series of tests, her doctor diagnosed her with stage 4 uterine cancer, bone cancer, and lung cancer. She had always thought that if she ever came down with cancer, she would not want to suffer through the prolonged and harsh treatments that might cure the cancer or keep it at bay. Fortunately for her, her family decided for her, and cancer treatments soon began. Radiation treatments started immediately, followed by even more brutal chemo treatments.

The doctors gave her little hope of ever being cancer-free. It would be something she had to live with and get treatment for continually. Eventually the cancer would get the best of her. Yet she clung to prayer and to Philippians 4:13, "I can do all things through him who strengthens me." After an incredible journey of weakness through the cancer treatments, it amazed the doctor to find no cancer in her body. He called her a *miracle*. God showed Himself strong in Lucinda, but God also used Lucinda's suffering to exercise and strengthen her faith. She now enjoys every day of life, knowing how quickly it could end. Her relationship with God is deeper and her faith is stronger.

Trials, tribulations, hardships, and suffering are spiritual exercises. Paul used athletic analogies often in his writings. In Romans 5:3–5, he wrote about this principle of spiritual exercise, "Not only that, but we rejoice in our sufferings, knowing that suffering produces endurance, and endurance produces character, and character produces hope, and hope does not put us to shame, because God's love has been poured into our hearts through the Holy Spirit who has been given to us." The word Paul uses for *suffering* in these verses comes from a root word meaning to *crush, press, compress,* or *squeeze*. Paul and other New Testament writers use the word to describe tribulation, trouble, affliction, or persecution.

Notice what Paul says about these sufferings. He said we should rejoice in them since they bring about endurance. I know it is hard to rejoice when in the middle of the pain of spiritual exercise, but in the end, we can rejoice in the endurance, strength, and patience that come from the trials we have faced. We can rejoice in spiritual growth.

James writes about this spiritual growth as well in James 1:2–4, "Count it all joy, my brothers, when you meet trials of various kinds, for you know that the testing of your faith produces steadfastness. And let steadfastness have its full effect, that you may be perfect and complete, lacking in nothing." James uses a different word to describe *trials* and *testing* than Paul uses, but the resulting *steadfastness* is the same as the *endurance* about which Paul writes. James also calls on us to rejoice, knowing that through our times of testing, we will grow stronger spiritually.

I have never been a world-class athlete although I have always loved playing sports. I have never been a bodybuilder although I have, at various times, lifted weights for strength training. In high school, I ran cross-country, played some basketball, did much biking on my ten-speed, and often went hiking in the mountains of Colorado. My athleticism, being mediocre, was never good enough to make me the best at the athletic events in which I competed. Still I have always enjoyed pitting my speed, strength, and skills against others.

I remember a time when serving in the US Marine Corps. I was on deployment in the Mediterranean, doing amphibious exercises with our NATO allies. As a Marine, my ship-board duties were light. There was not much to do until we hit the beach for a training exercise.

After a couple of months into the six-month tour, I felt flabby in my muscles. I looked down at my midsection and saw something protruding from my beltline. It was belly fat! It was shocking! I had never in my life seen such a thing! This would not do. I was determined to start working out in the small weight room on the ship. I was there for at least an hour each day, using the few dumbbells and the bench to work out my arms, chest, back, and legs. Every day, I spent at least thirty minutes running circles on the small helicopter landing pad on the deck of the ship.

When I first started my effort to get back in shape, I was very sore. Every muscle I worked hurt. But I continued to work through the pain. I specifically remember one morning when I looked in the mirror and flexed my arms up in a *bodybuilder pose*. I had shoulder and lateral muscles that looked good! Although I had put myself through much pain to get these muscles, I rejoiced in my newfound strength. By the way, I lost the flab in my gut as well! Regardless of the cause of our trials and tribulations, God will use them to strengthen us spiritually and eliminate the spiritual flab we might accumulate due to the lack of using our spiritual muscles. Sometimes we go through life and all is good. We become set in the routine of the Christian life. We are faithful in church, singing the songs and giving our tithe. We read our Bible and pray. We might even lead Bible studies, teaching others. But in all our doing, there is something missing. There is a lack of fervor in our Christianity. We have accumulated spiritual flab! This is not uncommon. We have all been there and done that.

It will not be easy. It will hurt. The longer we have been on Christian autopilot and have allowed some spiritual flab to accumulate, the harder and longer the rebuilding process will be. Still we can and should rejoice in the rebuilding of spiritual strength. If you are going through such a rebuilding process right now, stand strong. One day you will look in the mirror of God's Word and see something glorious. You will see some spiritual muscle that was not present when your trial began. You will look back at the difficulty and rejoice in what God has done within you. You will rejoice in your sufferings and tribulations!

Chapter 9

God Uses Our Suffering to Purify Us

In January 1848, gold was found in the river at the site where John Sutter was having a water-powered sawmill built by James Marshall. This started the California gold rush, which was the largest mass migration in US history. During the rush, over 300,000 people made their way to California seeking their fortunes in gold.

Human beings have long been fascinated with precious metals such as gold and silver. Gold is first mentioned in Genesis 2:11–12, where the writer mentions the four rivers that divided from the river flowing out of Eden. In Genesis 13:2, we read that "Abram was very rich in livestock, in silver, and in gold." In Genesis 24, Abram's servant, when he was searching for a wife for Isaac, gave Rebekah gold jewelry as a gift for watering his livestock. Later we see that there was much gold used in both the tabernacle and the temple. When John writes of the New Jerusalem in Revelation 21, he writes of gold being one of the primary building materials in this city. Even the street was made of pure gold!

Gold, when it first comes out of the ground, is anything but pure. It is usually mixed with many impurities and must be separated from those impurities. The process of separation has changed over the years but still primarily involves heating the gold to a temperature of about 2,100 degrees Fahrenheit. This is called smelting. I know gold is just a soft metal. It has no feelings. But if it did, it would scream out in pain! "Ouch! It is too hot! Turn down the heat! I can't take this anymore!" But when the process is complete, the gold would take great satisfaction in the purity it now possessed.

Writers of scripture write much of the process of refining gold, often relating it to the refining of people in the fires of adversity. Job speaks of it while he is going through his period of trial and affliction. He says in his response to Eliphaz in Job 23:10, "But he knows the way that I take; when he has tried me, I shall come out as gold." Job considered the great suffering he faced as God refining him like one refined gold. Many other Old Testament writers use the gold refining analogy. Psalm 66:10, Proverbs 17:3, Isaiah 48:10, Zechariah 13:9, and Malachi 3:3 are just a few places in the Old Testament where the writers use this analogy.

In the New Testament, John writes of the refining of gold in his letter from God to the church at Laodicea in Revelation 3:18. God tells the church, "I counsel you to buy from me gold refined by fire, so that you may be rich, and white garments so that you may clothe yourself and the shame of your nakedness may not be seen, and salve to anoint your eyes, so that you may see." The idea in these words seems to be that the church at Laodicea needed some refining. They needed some persecution or some such affliction to bring them back to a place of purity.

Peter also uses this refining analogy in 1 Peter 1:6–7, "In this you rejoice, though now for a little while you have been grieved by various trials, so that the tested genuineness of your faith—more precious than gold that perishes though it is tested by fire—may be found to result in praise and glory and honor at the revelation of Jesus Christ." Peter is saying that we can rejoice in our coming imperishable inheritance, but in this life, our faith will be tested in the fires of adversity. He says this is a precious thing! And the result of the testing of our faith is to bring praise and glory to Jesus!

A long-time and dear friend of my wife and mine, Glennis, tragically learned about the fires of adversity. She and her husband met in Bible college and were married in 1976. About one year later, they had their first child, a beautiful baby girl. About one year later, they were blessed with a baby boy and then another boy two and a half years later. When their children were teenagers, they adopted a newborn baby boy.

Glennis was living an ideal life. She described it in these words, "Life was wonderful. We lived in Colorado, where we went hiking, fishing, and skiing. We made many beautiful memories as a family. We served faithfully in our church and, after much prayer decided to home educate our children. I headed the first Southern Colorado Homeschool Group for several years. As my daughter got older, we started a Tea Ministry that lasted for more than twenty years. We spoke, laughed, and cried with women as we shared our journey with Christ."

Glennis had no idea that her ideal life would soon take a tragic turn. Her oldest son Joshua, at only twenty years old, loved the Lord and had already served as a youth pastor and the pastor of a church. She states, "He was a delight to be around." On July 4, 1999, Joshua passed out while swimming at a lake and drowned. He was gone. Glennis said her "heart was ripped apart."

Life continued for Glennis, her husband, and the other children. The pain of losing her son never went away, but the family began to find a new sense of normal. Every year on July 4, they celebrated the holiday with her daughter and her family, which now included four precious grandchildren.

After one such celebration in 2018, she went home with her oldest granddaughter while her husband stayed at the daughter's home to do some landscaping. A few days after arriving home, Glennis received a phone call from her daughter, which would change her life forever. In her own words, "That day ended my life as I knew it. I would lose everything in the coming months." Her husband had molested a young child and then turned himself in to the police.

Glennis lost much in a short time. Her oldest son was gone. Her husband was not the man she had thought he was. Her marriage was over. She felt lost and lonely. Her previous ideal life was now anything but ideal. She clung to God's promise related to the psalmist in Psalm 121:3, "He will not let your foot be moved; he who keeps you will not slumber." She knew deep in her heart that God was watching over her.

Glennis knew further that God was at work purifying her through the unimaginable tragedy that had struck her and her family. She described the process this way, "When God takes us through the fire, He refines our life like gold that has been purified. But first we must endure the process. Fire is hot and at times it can hurt you. But fire is also useful in creating beautiful images when precious metals are purified. In His great love for us, He uses tragedy to purify us. Making us ready to meet Him and to live in His heavenly kingdom! The purification process is a part of His faithful love."

After years of being *purified in the fiery furnace*, God gave Glennis a new husband, Rod, whose wife had recently passed away from cancer. Rod loves her children and grandchildren as if they were his own. They minister together. They have plans to begin ministries for older women who find themselves alone and a ministry to encourage cancer patients.

Knowing Glennis as I do, I wonder to myself, *What is it that God needed to remove from her life through the process of purification?* I have no answer to that question. Glennis has no genuine answer to that question. But God knows. We may never know the full results of our purification this side of heaven, but we can rejoice, knowing that our Almighty God loved us enough to refine our lives and our character for our good and for His glory. We can rejoice, knowing that we are a bit more like Jesus and know Him more, having experienced the "fellowship of his suffering" (Philippians 3:10).

We may not know what God is doing in us through the purification process. But there is little doubt that sometimes as we go through life, we pick up many impurities along the way. Pride, greed, bad habits, the allure of fame or notoriety, and lust are just a few of the impurities we can pick up. Much like gold in the ground, our lives become mixed with the grime, dirt, and rocks of the world. And like gold, we do not shine like we should because of the impurities we have picked up. God uses the suffering brought on by the trials of life to purify us. He desires to remove the impurities so He can shine through our lives. He wants others to see Himself through us. But to do that, there might need to be some smelting. We might be heated in the furnace so that the impurities can be removed.

When you are in the middle of the fires of adversity, you may think much like gold would if it had feelings. "God, this hurts too much! I can't take this anymore! Please turn down the heat!" When life hurts and your world is crashing down around you, it is hard to think of the benefit of the refining process. You just want the pain to stop. But know that when this *smelting* process ends, you will be more pure and will better glorify the Lord. There will be less of you in the way so more of Jesus can shine through!

Chapter 10

God Uses Suffering to Steer Us Back on Course

We have all seen children pretend to steer a car on a toy steering wheel or even while sitting in an actual car in the driver's seat on Mom's or Dad's lap. They move the wheel back and forth exaggeratedly, trying to imitate what they have seen Mom or Dad do while driving. As they have watched others drive a car by moving the wheel back and forth, they repeat the movement. They did not know why. They just knew that is how it was done because Mom and Dad did it that way. They did not know that when Mom and Dad moved the wheel back and forth, they were doing so in order to keep the car going straight down the road.

When we begin driving, we soon realize that a vehicle will not drive straight by itself. The driver must guide it. There are several reasons the car might drift to one side of the road or the other. It certainly could be driver inattention. If we stare too long at some beautiful scenery or an amazing sight, the car will tend to drift in that direction. Once we get our attention back on the road, we must make the proper correction on the steering wheel to get the car back on course.

The wind can also cause a vehicle to drift. A vehicle will always drift in the same direction the wind is blowing. A strong crosswind on the highway will cause the driver to work hard and continually to keep the car on course. I remember riding a motorcycle through the Oklahoma panhandle in 1994 on my way to New Mexico. There arose a terrible dust storm driven by a powerful wind. The area I was in when the wind hit was a very isolated stretch of highway. There was no place to stop and get out of the wind. I kept on riding. The wind was so strong I had to lean the motorcycle like I was going through a sharp curve, just to keep it going straight.

Sometimes it is simply the slope of the road that will cause a vehicle to drift in the slope's direction. Most highways are built at a slight slant to the side of the road to keep water from puddling on the road. This slope will cause a vehicle to drift toward the slope, and the wary driver must continually correct this drift using the steering wheel.

Whether it be driver inattention, windy weather, or road conditions, a vehicle will drift off the road if the driver is not continually correcting course using the steering wheel. The same is true in life. Sometimes we drift off course because we are not paying attention. We get distracted by the glitz and glamor of life. We get caught up in the things of the world. We lose our focus on the path ahead and we drift off course.

This happened to a companion and friend of Paul the Apostle. His name was Demas. We know little about Demas. He is mentioned as a fellow worker, along with Luke, Mark, Aristarchus, and Epaphras in Philemon 1:23–24. In Colossians, Paul mentions Demas, along with Luke, as sending his greeting to the Colossians. But then, near the end of Paul's life, while he was in prison awaiting execution,

Paul's relationship with Demas had taken a sad turn. In 2 Timothy 4:10, Paul wrote Demas abandoned him because of his love for the world. Demas strayed off course because his attention was on things of the world.

Let us not judge Demas too harshly, for we have all been there. We have all allowed the lust of the flesh, the lust of the eyes, and the pride of life to distract us from the path God has for us. Sometimes we might even become distracted by something that is good. We allow the good to take priority over what is best.

When I was serving on active duty in the US Marine Corps at Camp Lejeune in North Carolina, we attended a church in town outside of the base. I spent a lot of time away from home on exercises, operations, and deployments. When I was home, I was very active in the church where we were members. Randy, the pastor of the church, asked me to lunch one day. In my mind, I thought he would commend me for all I was doing in the church. Instead, he rebuked me for not spending enough time with my small family when I was home. I have strayed off course from what was most important.

In this hectic world in which we live, it is easy to stray off course. When we do, God will sometimes use trials, tribulations, and suffering to steer us back on course. Psalm 119:67 states, "Before I was afflicted I went astray, but now I keep your word." The word *astray* means that one sins or commits an error even inadvertently. The psalmist realized that when he went astray, it was the affliction that brought him back on course to keep God's Word.

While we do occasionally stray off course inadvertently, there are other times we willfully seek that which is contrary to God's ways. We pursue material things instead of the spiritual ones. We seek pleasure in sin instead of finding our joy in the Lord. Just like we, as earthly parents, will discipline our children, so our heavenly Father may need to discipline us to steer us back on course. We do not discipline our children out of anger or spite but to correct them. As followers of Christ, if we willfully get off the course God has for us, He will lovingly try to steer us back on course.

When Moses was relaying God's commandments to the people of Israel, he spoke these words in Deuteronomy 8:5, "Know then in your heart that, as a man disciplines his son, the LORD your God disciplines you." He told them that if they were not in obedience to God's commandments, He would discipline them. There are many examples of this discipline found in Israel's history.

The book of Judges tells us repeatedly that Israel "did what was evil in the sight of the LORD. They forgot the LORD their God and served the Baals and the Asheroth" (Judges 3:7). Then when they had enough of being disciplined and the suffering it entailed, they cried out to God and God raised up a deliverer, a judge, to deliver them. It is of note in Judges that it was often God who strengthened the enemy of Israel, giving them the opportunity to conquer His people. God used the enemies of Israel to discipline His people. He used Israel's enemies to make a course correction.

We may stray off course because of our lack of attention. We may be in a place of willful rebellion against God's ways. Or we may become distracted by things and material possessions. God may use some difficulty to remove those distractions.

I started my career with the Federal Bureau of Prisons in 1991 at the Medical Center for Federal Prisoners in Springfield, Missouri. In 1995, I transferred to the Supermax Federal Prison in Florence, Colorado. We spent five years there, transferring back to Springfield in 2000 to finish out my career. At the time of that transfer, we had six children. We looked for a home to buy with some land for our large family. One of the first places we looked at was the home we still occupy. It is a large farmhouse on four acres. We lowballed the owner with our first offer, which he rejected.

We continued to search the market but found nothing as perfect for us as that place. Finally, when we could find nothing to meet our needs, we went back to see if we could make a deal on the home and the four acres. One of the sticking points was that there were three outbuildings, which the owner wanted to keep. This would not have been such a big deal, except that the proposed property line would be literally on the front edge of a thirty-five-foot-by-seventy-foot barn. This was not OK with me. I wanted the buildings, especially the enormous barn.

We made a final offer for the place. We offered the owner his full asking price, but only if he would include all three outbuildings with twenty to thirty feet of space past the buildings as the new property line. Our realtor said there was no way he would accept our offer, but he did! We closed on the place and moved in a few weeks later in October 2002. In December 2002, we had some strange weather which resulted in a wintertime EF1 tornado. Our place was the first place to be hit. The house sustained a bit of damage to the roof and windows but remained sturdy and standing. However, the large barn I had fought so hard for was completely demolished. There was nothing left standing but two support posts in the middle of the barn.

I had strayed off course by attaching too much desire to that barn. I wanted it. I had to have it. I had grand plans for it. God steered my thinking back on course by taking the barn!

When you are going through a time of trial and tribulation, one question you should ask yourself is "Have I strayed off course in my Christian walk?" You should examine your life to see if you may have inadvertently directed your attention to that which may be good but is not the best. You may be placing greater value on the things of the world instead of your relationship with God. You may have strayed off course in pursuit of worldly pleasures. If this is the case, thank God that He loves you enough to steer you back on course. Purpose in your heart that you will keep your eyes on the road and make minor corrections to stay on the course He sets for you.

Chapter 11

God Uses Our Suffering to Reveal Our Character

A few months after Sylvia and I were married, Dave and Bev, who had been married a few months longer than us, invited us to their apartment for a dinner party. There were four other couples besides us. In the early months of their life together, Dave and Bev had only a few meals they made for dinner repeatedly. One of those meals was lasagna. We were told with our invitation that lasagna would be on the menu for the dinner party.

This excited me. I really liked a good lasagna, and I figured that if Bev had been making lasagna on a weekly basis for several months, she would be an expert at lasagna making. My mouth watered just thinking about the dinner to come. The night arrived for the dinner, and when we entered their apartment, the aroma of garlic, cheese, and tomato sauce permeated the air. My stomach rumbled in anticipation.

When the dinner was ready, we all sat at the table, and Bev brought out the lasagna. She placed the large pan of lasagna on the table and cut it into squares. She placed a spatula under the first piece to serve it. As she lifted the spatula, the entire piece fell right back into the pan. Bev had forgotten to put noodles in her lasagna! We all politely tried to reign in our laughter, but it was nearly impossible. Bev was devastated but calmly picked up the pan of lasagna-like and went back to the kitchen. She boiled a pot of spaghetti noodles, which she brought out with the lasagna mix. We scooped the lasagna mix over the spaghetti noodles and had a fine meal.

Bev's pan of sauce, cheese, meat, and spices looked like a lasagna. It smelled like a lasagna. It even tasted like a lasagna. But it was not a lasagna. It took cutting into the mixture before we discovered the truth about what was inside. There was one very necessary ingredient that was still needed to make it a true lasagna through and through. It needed lasagna noodles to hold the other ingredients together into a true lasagna.

Sometimes as we go through life, we get busy with the routine and sometimes mundane activities that make up our daily existence. We get up in the morning and go through our normal routine. We take the kids to school, go to work, eat lunch, come home, eat dinner, watch TV, and then get ready for bed to do it all over again. In all the busyness of life, we neglect to give God any real time during our day. This might last for days, and for some, it could last weeks, months, or years.

As we become spiritually weak, God must sometimes put us in situations where we must examine what is really on the inside. It may take *cutting* open the lasagna of our life so we can see if the noodles are present to hold everything else together. This cutting open may take various forms or come in varying degrees. It could be severe or it could be very mild. But the purpose is to show us what we are like on the inside so we will get back to building the proper *noodles* into the lasagna of our lives.

I know it is difficult to think that God might bring us into a place of trial or tribulation simply to test our character. But if our goal and destiny are to be like Jesus, the trials of life are sometimes necessary to show us where we are on our journey. We become very good at hiding who we are deep down from people around us and even from ourselves. We talk the Christian talk, go to church, give our tithes, sing the songs, and everything seems to be good in life. It may take God putting us into a place of suffering so that we will take an inventory of our character. We can then see what is missing and take steps to get back into a pattern of Christian growth instead of pretense.

In chapter 8, we looked briefly at Romans 5:3–5. We noted we should rejoice in our sufferings because *suffering produces endurance.* But look at what comes from that suffering/endurance-producing combination. Paul writes that "endurance produces character." The Greek word for *character* here indicates that it is proven through experience. It is suffering that leads to this proven character.

This is what happened to Job throughout his ordeal with loss and suffering. His character was proven to Satan. But his character was also proven to himself. Job also discovered an area of his faith that was a bit lacking, which only added to his character-building suffering. Job 42:5–6 says, "I had heard of you by the hearing of the ear, but now my eye sees you; therefore I despise myself, and repent in dust and ashes." Job had great faith in the God he had only heard about. His picture of God through his hearing was less than what it should have been. Through his suffering, he saw God at work. His clearer picture of God gave him a clearer picture of himself. This clearer picture caused him to realize how insignificant he was when compared to God Almighty.

I do not know exactly what God is trying to do in and through you amid your suffering. But I know He may be trying to help you see your character more clearly. In the middle of your trials and tribulations, spend some time in introspection. Look into your heart and see what has been exposed through the *cutting* of the lasagna of your life. As you see what is deep inside, you may realize there are some *noodles* missing from your lasagna. Take time then to pray and ask God to help you develop a more proven character through your time of difficulty. This is a prayer God loves to hear!

Chapter 12

God Uses Our Suffering to Accomplish His Plans

This purpose might rub some people the wrong way. If God uses our suffering to accomplish His plans, then is God the author of our suffering? No, but God can and will use our sufferings to accomplish His plan for us and those around us.

In chapter 3, we looked a bit at the suffering of Joseph that was caused by the jealousy of his brothers. They sinned and Joseph paid the price through hardship and trial. We will now look at Joseph's story from the standpoint of the purpose of his suffering.

Here is a recap of the amazing journey of Joseph in Genesis 37–50. He was a seventeen-year-old boy who was sold into slavery by his brothers. He had committed no sin, yet because of their jealousy, he ended up in Egypt as a slave to Potiphar. God blessed Joseph in his work for Potiphar, and Joseph was put in charge of caring for Potiphar's estate. Potiphar's wife attempted to seduce Joseph. As an honorable young man, he refused her advances. On her last attempt,

Joseph fled the scene, leaving his garment in her grasping hands. She then cried, "Rape!" and they threw Joseph into prison.

God again blessed Joseph, and he ended up running the prison facility, answering only to the prison keeper. During his confinement, two of the Pharaoh's servants, his cupbearer, and his baker, were imprisoned. One day, they both had dreams that troubled them. Joseph interpreted their dreams. Joseph's interpretations were spot on! The Pharaoh hanged the baker and restored the cupbearer to his position in the court. The cupbearer had promised to tell the Pharaoh about Joseph but forgot to do so. Joseph spent two more years in prison.

Then the Pharaoh had a couple of very troubling dreams. No one could interpret his dreams. Finally, the cupbearer remembered Joseph and told the Pharaoh about his incredible ability to interpret dreams. They brought Joseph before the Pharaoh. He interpreted the dreams. Both pointed to a time of great famine in the land. Joseph boldly gave the Pharaoh advice on how to prepare for the famine so that the nation would survive the drought. Because of Joseph's wisdom, the Pharaoh made Joseph the overseer of the proposed plan. Joseph ended up being second in command of the entire nation, answering only to the Pharaoh. Joseph superbly managed the national response to the drought. Egypt became a place of salvation for many other nations and peoples, including Joseph's own family.

Joseph, as a seventeen-year-old boy, unwisely told his family about his dreams that they would one day bow down to him. This led to his captivity and eventually to his rise to power in Egypt. Then we read an ironic twist of fate in Genesis 42:6, "Now Joseph was governor over the land. He was the one who sold to all the people of the land. And Joseph's brothers came and bowed themselves before him with their faces to the ground." Joseph's dream had come true. His brothers bowed down to him!

When Joseph finally revealed himself to his brothers, he made a profound statement, found in Genesis 50:20. He said, "As for you, you meant evil against me, but God meant it for good, to bring it about that many people should be kept alive, as they are today."

God did not cause Joseph's hardship and suffering. His suffering had two causes. The first was his own youthful lack of wisdom (telling his family about dreams, which he should have kept to himself). The second was the jealousy his dreams caused in his brothers. Yet God had a plan and used Joseph's hardship to bring about His plan.

We can look back and see how God used the suffering in Joseph's life to bring about His plans for the people of Israel. We can look back and see how God used tragedy and suffering in the lives of many biblical characters and in the lives of people throughout history. But when we are in the middle of our own tragedy, hardship, and suffering, it is much harder to see God's hand at work. It is hard to see past the pain. This was true in the lives of Gabe and Bethany.

Over the course of three and a half years, they suffered tremendous pain and tragedy in their family. Within six months, two of their children had limbs amputated in accidents. One year later, Bethany miscarried their unborn child. Six months later, Bethany walked in to find their two-year-old foster child dead in his crib. Bethany described their suffering this way, "So much trauma. I lost myself several times through it all. In the exhaustion and pain during the dark of night and much more through many waking hours of daylight, the losses and suffering were constant companions."

Yet even in her dark times, Bethany knew God was with her family. She knew in her heart that the suffering they faced had to be part of God's plan. She did not know what that plan was, but she knew God was working His plan in their lives. Bethany puts it this way, "There were times of peace walking through it all. I felt

God more deeply at times than I have ever known. I knew He was there in the blackness and chaos of it all, silently in step with me, sometimes feeling His presence at my back, guarding my trail; other times at my side to make sure I did not falter in my steps; or in front of me, guiding me along a particularly treacherous path. Directing me in His way … in His will."

Bethany and Gabe have learned much through their trials, and they are still learning. One of the greatest lessons they are learning is to trust God to accomplish His will in their lives through tragedy and suffering. She told me she learned "a true and better understanding of what we call 'fear of the Lord.' That nothing, nothing, will stand in His way to accomplish His purpose in me and in His plans for the world. This comes with a heavy price at times, pruning dead things and even healthy pieces in order for me to flourish and grow more. Maiming and sickness, chaos, loss, and even death … is not too small a price to pay for His will to be accomplished."

God Almighty is a master at taking the tragedy of life and turning it into something beautiful and beneficial. He is the potter who can take a messed-up lump of clay and shape it into a useful vessel. He is the mechanic who can take a wrecked and dilapidated vehicle and turn it into a well-tuned motor vehicle. He can take the worst of life's situations and make them into something beautiful and victorious.

It matters not what caused the tragedy and brought about hardship and suffering. It matters not how desperate or ugly the situation may be. God is not limited by what has happened or how it happened. We must simply trust Him and allow Him to do the work only He can do. He may very well use your suffering to accomplish big plans in your life and the lives of those around you.

Chapter 13

God Uses Our Suffering to Prepare Us for His Glory

There have been several times in my life I have fasted. This fasting occurred for various reasons. The first such occasion was when I was sixteen years old, living in Thornton, Colorado. During the summer of 1976, I was part of the Outward Bound wilderness program in the mountains of Colorado. It was a three-week course, wherein I and ten other young men aged sixteen to twenty learned hiking, climbing, and other wilderness skills.

The program consisted of four expeditions. The first was a six-day training expedition. We learned the basics of how to pack our gear, climb and hike in rough terrain, and use a compass and a map for land navigation. The second expedition lasted eight days. Our packs were heavier since we were to be out in the mountains longer. We covered a lot of terrain and climbed several amazing peaks during this second expedition.

The third expedition was a solo expedition. The instructor gave us boundaries near a crystal-clear stream for drinking water.

We were to stay within our boundaries with nothing but a shelter, a book to read, a canteen for drinking water, and the essentials for nature's business. Here I was, a sixteen-year-old teenage boy, who just prior to leaving for this course ate three chocolate pies in two days, thanks to my mother! I had to go three full days with no food. I made it through the three-day solo in fine fashion, but when it was over, I was starving!

When all the students were back together at base camp, I noticed a pen full of rather large rabbits. I was about to ask about getting something to eat when the instructor pointed to the pen of rabbits and said, "There's dinner, boys!" I had never butchered or eaten a rabbit, but I figured out quickly how to butcher, clean, cut up, and roast my rabbit. It seemed to be the best-tasting meal I have ever had in my life.

When we are starving, we appreciate food much more than when we are eating three good meals per day. It is the same with water. To the person who is very thirsty, water is more valuable than anything. I have seen several Western movies over the years where a character in the movie must pass through a barren desert with no water. By the time he finally makes it to water, he wants it more than anything else including food.

Our trials, tribulations, difficulties, and hardships, along with the accompanying suffering, do the same for our souls. They make us long for heaven in the same way that a hungry person longs for food and a thirsty person longs for water. Paul the Apostle suffered much in his life. He recounts some of his hardships when writing to the church at Corinth, in 2 Corinthians 11:24–28, "Five times I received at the hands of the Jews the forty lashes less one. Three times I was beaten with rods. Once I was stoned. Three times I was shipwrecked; a night and a day I was adrift at sea; on frequent journeys, in danger from rivers, danger from robbers, danger from my own people, danger from Gentiles, danger in the city, danger in the wilderness, danger at sea, danger from false brothers; in toil and hardship, through many a sleepless night, in hunger and thirst, often without food, in cold and exposure. And, apart from other things, there is the daily pressure on me of my anxiety for all the churches."

When Paul writes anything about suffering, he writes with authority born from great personal experience. He writes in Romans 8:18, "For I consider that the sufferings of this present time are not worth comparing with the glory that is to be revealed to us." In 2 Corinthians 4:17, he puts it this way, "For this light momentary affliction is preparing for us an eternal weight of glory beyond all comparison." While Paul was imprisoned in Rome, he thought much about going home to be with the Lord. He told the church at Philippi of his longing in Philippians 1:23–24, "I am hard pressed between the two. My desire is to depart and be with Christ, for that is far better. But to remain in the flesh is more necessary on your account." He was ready to go to his heavenly home but willing to stay and serve God by continuing his mission of spreading the gospel and growing the churches.

Consider the story of Ben and Christina. Their nine-month-old daughter Caitlin was a perfectly healthy, growing, and precious little girl. On December 17, 2015, Christina's mother and father found little Caitlin unresponsive in bed. They performed CPR while awaiting the paramedics. At the local hospital, they revived her tiny heart, but Caitlin could not breathe on her own. Two days later, a brain specialist ran a series of tests and declared that there was no brain activity. Ben and Christina made the agonizing decision to take their baby off life support. They gathered with the other children in the family to say their last goodbyes. Ben and Christina removed life support and held their precious baby as she took her last breath.

The grief and pain they experienced is something from which no man or woman can ever fully heal. The pain runs so deep that it will always be a part of them. To cope with their loss, they have chosen as a family to keep baby Caitlin in their lives by including a picture of her in every family photo they take. On the day of her heavenly birthday, they celebrate with a special family activity to establish joyful memories.

Christina said they long for the day when Revelation 21:4 becomes reality. "He will wipe away every tear from their eyes, and death shall be no more, neither shall there be mourning, nor crying, nor pain anymore, for the former things have passed away." They are confident that one day, they will be reunited with their precious Caitlin.

Is there some purpose in your suffering? Like Paul and like Ben and Christina, God wants to develop in you a hunger for heaven. He wants you to yearn for the eternity that awaits those who trust in Him. When you are in the most difficult times of your life, allow the suffering to grow in you a hunger for the glory of heaven. You have likely thought like I have when in the middle of hardship. "Lord, if you were to come back in the next couple of minutes, I would be so very excited to see you!" When you are suffering in the trials of your life, I would suggest a prayer like this, "Lord, I am hurting. I am confused. I am tired. But I pray you will turn my pain into a hunger to see you. I pray you will make me long for the glories of heaven. I am ready to go home but willing to stay here and serve you even though I might suffer more pain."

Chapter 14

God Uses Our Suffering to Draw Our Attention Back to Him

In the fall of 1983, I was twenty-three years old and managing a Wendy's restaurant in Denver, Colorado. The store was in a rough part of town. The area was so bad that we hired an armed security guard. He would sit in our restaurant from 6:00 p.m. until after we closed, and I dropped our daily deposit in the bank's night deposit box.

One evening, at about 9:00 p.m., my employees were doing some preclosing work. I had about nine customers in the dining area, including a couple of young men about twenty years old or so, who were sitting near a door. They were laughing and having a good time. Suddenly the security guard completely lost it, pulled out his .38 Special, and fired two shots at the young men sitting next to the door. Whoa! I yelled out to my employees, "Get in the back! Call 911!"

Meanwhile, I ran out to lend aid to the two young men, whom I assumed had been shot. As I rounded the corner into the dining area, I noticed several things in an instant. The security guard missed both of his shots! The other customers were diving to the floor and scrambling for cover. The young men were running down the street as fast as they could. The guard was stepping through the door and was aiming at their backs! Without thinking, I busted through the door and yelled, "Stop!" He did not fire the weapon at the two young men. Instead, he turned completely around and aimed the pistol right in my face! That pistol was less than twelve inches from my eyes.

I could see smoke still coming from the barrel. I could see his finger on the trigger with the hammer about halfway back. But mostly, I saw the black hole in the barrel. A .38 Special is not a large caliber weapon, but that black hole looked like a vast tunnel to me! It looked like I could walk into it and become lost. My eyes were so focused on that hole that nothing else in my life mattered. No temptation to sin could have averted my eyes. The problems of the world meant nothing to me. My universe at that moment was in that black hole.

Eventually, without knowing what I was doing, I talked him into handing me the gun. It seemed like an eternity but was probably only seconds. About the time I had the gun in my possession, the police pulled up with the two young men with them. There were several hours of interviews with me, my employees, and the other customers. I can still remember that event like it was yesterday. But over the years, the Lord taught me some valuable lessons from that terrifying ordeal.

He showed me that when my focus on Him is strong, the things of this world become dimmer. Temptations to sin have less pull when we focus on Him. Problems, hardships, difficulties, and suffering may still be present, but we notice them less when we are focused on Him. There is a physiological precedent for this phenomenon. Our eyes can only focus on one object at a time. Anyone who has ever fired a rifle with iron sights knows this well. One cannot focus on the target while focusing on the front or rear sight. You learn to focus on the front sight while leaving the target and the rear sight a bit blurry. When one's focus is true, one can usually hit the target.

In our Christian life, our struggles tend to capture our attention in the moment. The cause of our hardship and suffering draws our focus. Whether or not we are conscious of it, the object of our pain often becomes the object of our spiritual focus. In the Christian life, though it feels natural, it ought not to be. Our primary focus should always be the Lord, not our hardships, problems, or sufferings.

A dear friend Rod learned this lesson. Rod had always been a rather optimistic and upbeat guy. He faced life's struggles head-on, knowing that God would work it all out. However, on June 1, 2020, Rod found himself on a journey of suffering that left him feeling *washed ashore in utter ruins.*

As he stepped up into his house carrying a bag of groceries, his left leg completely gave out on him. He required help to get into the house. Later his right leg lost all strength, and he began to experience extreme pain in his back. Soon he was completely bound to a wheelchair to get around. He felt in chaos, both emotionally and spiritually. He described it like this, "I felt as though I had lost a part of myself, and my once-positive outlook was replaced with feelings of despair and hopelessness."

Rod was in constant pain and bound to a wheelchair. Rod had always been a man of faith, allowing his faith in God to guide him through difficult situations, but now he felt lost and abandoned. This spiritual and emotional struggle continued for almost two years.

Then on Easter Sunday, he woke up, and something changed inside of him. Rod felt a sense of renewal and joy that had been absent for nearly two years. He said, "I felt a sense of clarity and purpose I had not experienced in almost two years." He knew beyond any shadow of a doubt that Jesus was alive. Jesus had risen from the grave! It was like he knew once and for all that God loved him and had a plan for his life.

Here is Rod's testimony in his own words:

> Since that day, both physically and spiritually, I have been healed. It hasn't been an easy journey, but I have learned to trust God's plan for my life, even when it takes me to dark and difficult places. I have come to realize that He gives and takes away, but His love and His grace remain constant. And through it all, He is molding me and shaping me for His purpose and His glory. I have learned that no matter what challenges we face in life, God is always with us, guiding us and renewing us day by day. He is the source of our strength and our hope, and He can turn even the darkest moments into something beautiful and redemptive. I have learned to praise His name in all things, to trust in His plan for my life, and to be a willing vessel for His glory. Through my struggles and my pain, I have come to realize that all things work together for the good of those who are chosen in Him. And for that, I am forever grateful.

When Rod was in the middle of his pain and suffering, his focus was on the pain and suffering. When he awoke on that Easter morning, his focus changed. He focused on the Savior, the Risen One! His pain and suffering did not leave immediately, but it was no longer the object of his focus. Once his focus changed, his attitude and outlook on life changed as well.

The lesson Rod learned is the same one Peter learned in one of the most fascinating stories in the Bible. Jesus had just fed over five thousand people with five loaves of bread and two fish. He sent the disciples to sail to the other side of the sea while He went up to the mountain to pray. In the wee hours of the morning, the disciples were struggling with the boat because of the wind and the choppy seas. Jesus, having finished his prayer time, came out to meet them, walking on top of the water.

The disciples saw Him, and knowing that men could not walk on water, they thought it was a ghost. Jesus calmed them by calling out, "Take heart; it is I. Do not be afraid" (Matthew 14:27). Then Peter, being the impetuous one he was, said, "Lord, if it is you, command me to come to you on the water" (Matthew 14:28). Matthew then records the amazing event this way in Matthew 14:29–31, "He said, 'Come.' So Peter got out of the boat and walked on the water and came to Jesus. But when he saw the wind, he was afraid, and beginning to sink he cried out, 'Lord, save me.' Jesus immediately reached out his hand and took hold of him, saying to him, 'O you of little faith, why did you doubt?'"

Peter, upon recognizing the Lord, jumped out of the boat and became the second person in the earth's history to walk on water! Remember that the seas were choppy because of the wind. So Peter would have been riding the waves up and down as he made his way to Jesus. The storm was all around him. The wind was blowing, and the waves were crashing. Peter paid no attention to any of it. He was walking on top of the water on his way to Jesus! As long as his eyes were on Jesus, the storm was of little consequence. He had no fear of the storm. But when he took his eyes off Jesus and looked at the waves, he became afraid. It was then that the storm threatened to overwhelm him.

We all need to learn the lesson Rod and Peter learned. When we focus our spiritual eyes on Jesus, the storms do not go away. The suffering does not cease, and the pain is still there. But when we focus on Jesus, all that is around us, no matter how bad it may seem to be, dims compared to our view of the Lord. I believe the Lord uses our suffering to draw our attention back to Him.

After the murder of my brother and his wife, our lives were chaotic and filled with grief and suffering. Our focus became simply putting one foot in front of the other. "Just do the next thing" became our motto. While searching for answers to my question, "Why me, Lord?", I found a passage of scripture that lifted me up and gave me great hope: Lamentations 3.

At the beginning of the chapter, the prophet Jeremiah describes the great pain he is suffering for his people. Jerusalem had fallen. The temple had been destroyed. The people were in captivity. Jeremiah, presumably the author of Lamentations, wrote a poem of lament to encourage the people to confess their sins and return to the Lord. I would encourage you to take some time now to read Lamentations 3, particularly, verses 1–23. Keep in mind as you read, Jeremiah uses *he* and *him* to refer to God. The *I* and *my* refer to himself.

In the first twenty verses of chapter 3, the prophet uses some very expressive figures of speech to describe the pain he feels. Lamentations 3:4 says, "He has made my flesh and my skin waste away; he has broken my bones." Lamentations 3:7 states, "He has walled me about so that I cannot escape; he has made my chains heavy." Lamentations 3:10 says, "He is a bear lying in wait for me, a lion in hiding." Lamentations 3:13 states, "He drove into my kidneys the arrows of his quiver." Keep in mind that Jeremiah is using figurative language to describe his pain. It is not his view of God!

After twenty verses describing his deep suffering, Jeremiah changes his tune. Lamentations 3:21 says, "But this I call to mind, and therefore I have hope." His lamentation brings him to a place of remembrance. His suffering caused him to remember something! It caused him to turn his gaze back to the Lord. This remembering brought him hope. Here is what he remembered in Lamentations 3:22–23, "The steadfast love of the LORD never ceases; his mercies never come to an end; they are new every morning; great is your faithfulness."

Jeremiah is saying, "I am suffering. My pain is significant. But my suffering and pain have caused me to remember the Lord. I remember that His love never ceases and that His mercies never come to an end. I remember His mercies are new with every morning. And I remember God is faithful!" Jeremiah took his eyes off the hardship, pain, and suffering and turned his focus to the one who is greater than all the storms. He remembered God, and in his remembrance of who God is, he found hope!

Whatever it is you are going through and no matter how much it hurts, God wants to use your suffering to turn your attention and focus back to him. He wants you to remember Him. Regardless of how much it hurts, there is hope. His great love and mercies are new every morning. His great love and mercies are also new in every mourning. He is faithful. He will never fail you. Turn to Him and find hope in your suffering.

It does not matter what has caused your hardship, trial, tribulation, difficulty, pain, or suffering. You may be suffering through the consequences of some bad choices. You may be suffering because of the sin and evil of another person. Maybe you are under attack by the enemy of all that is good and godly. Perhaps you have been caught up in the natural turmoil and chaos of this fallen world. Whatever the cause, "The steadfast love of the LORD never ceases;

his mercies never come to an end; they are new every morning; And He is faithful!"

To focus on the Lord's love, mercy, and faithfulness does not make the pain go away. It does not make the suffering stop. But as you focus on the Lord, the things of this earth will grow dim by comparison. Read or sing the words of the first verse and chorus of this great old hymn by Helen H. Lemmel:

> O soul are you weary and troubled
> No light in the darkness you see
> There's light for a look at the Savior
> And life more abundant and free.
> Turn your eyes upon Jesus
> Look full in his wonderful face
> And the things of earth will grow strangely dim
> In the light of his glory and grace.

If you are going through great hardship right now and are suffering under a heavy load of care, remember Jesus. Turn your eyes to Jesus. Cry out to Him. Ask Him to help you see His love, mercy, and faithfulness.

Summary and Closing Thoughts

We will all face trials, tribulations, troubles, hardships, hard times, afflictions, storms, and sufferings. This is not what God intended for His creation, but when Adam and Eve sinned, the curse of sin began to wreak havoc on all that God created. Yet God was not defeated by this. He began a process of redemption that runs from Genesis to Revelation. He will one day completely redeem His people and His creation from the ravages of sin and the destruction it has brought.

Although the suffering we experience is not what God intended for mankind, it is where we now live. It is commonplace and affects us all. We suffer because of our own sinfulness and foolishness, the sin of other people, the enemy of God and all that is good, the storms that fall on everyone, and simply because we live in a fallen world. One or more of these has caused any suffering you experience.

Regardless of the cause of our suffering, God can and will use our suffering. He will give purpose to our suffering. He will use our sufferings to show Himself strong in us, strengthen us, purify us, steer us back on course, reveal our character, accomplish His plans, and prepare us for His glory. If you cannot connect your suffering to any of these purposes, you can without a doubt find purpose in the ultimate purpose mentioned in chapter 14: God will always desire our sufferings to draw our attention to Him.

I have preached the sermon, on which this book is based, several times in many venues. Every time I have preached this message, I am touched by the response of those who hear it. It is a message that speaks to us all because we all go through hard times in life. Every time I have preached this message, the Lord has prompted me to put it all down into a book. The Lord has given me the ability to speak the Word, and I am confident in that ability. But it took me some time to come to the place where I felt confident enough to write it all down. Still, in obedience to the Lord's calling in my life, I have shared now in print the message God gave me about trials, sufferings, and hardships in life.

I wrote this book from a biblical perspective and primarily for those who are followers of Jesus. However, I believe anyone who is suffering hardship can read this book and find answers. If you have read this book and have never come to know Jesus personally, I pray you will consider your spiritual state. Life is short. There is no guarantee you will live another day. We like to think we will live a long, happy life, and some do. But we all know those who did not.

Jesus loves you! He died on a cross for you. He was buried and came out of His grave three days later. He is alive! He wants to walk through life with you. Reach out to me. I would be happy to share with you the life-changing truth of the Gospel of Jesus.

It is my prayer, after reading this book, that you have found some answers to the question of your heart, "Why me, Lord?" I pray that the answers you have found will encourage you to keep taking the next step in your life. Life is challenging. Trouble will come. You will suffer pain, heartache, and brokenness in this life—there is no escaping it. But there is encouragement and hope in the answers found in God's Word, the Holy Bible. May God richly bless you!